# GASB Statement No. 34 Implementation Recommendations For School Districts

Authored by ASBO International
Accounting, Auditing and Budgeting Committee
Subcommittee on GASB Statement No. 34
Implementation

Published in partnership with the
Association of School Business Officials International

ScarecrowEducation
Lanham, Maryland • Toronto • Oxford
2000

Published in partnership with
the Association of School Business Officials International

Published in the United States of America
by ScarecrowEducation
An imprint of The Rowman & Littlefield Publishing Group, Inc
4501 Forbes Boulevard, Suite 200, Lanham, Maryland 20706
www.scarecroweducation.com

PO Box 317
Oxford
OX2 9RU, UK



British Library Cataloguing in Publication Information Available

Library of Congress Cataloging-in-Publication Data Available

ISBN 978-1-57886-067-8

Reprinted by ScarecrowEducation

™ The paper used in this publication meets the minimum requirements of American National Standard for Information Sciences—Permanence of Paper for Printed Library Materials, ANSI/NISO Z39.48-1992.
Manufactured in the United States of America.

## Table of Contents

# Introduction

After more than 10 years of deliberation and debate with substantial controversy and compromise along the way, the Governmental Accounting Standards Board (GASB) on June 30, 1999, unanimously approved GASB Statement No. 34, *Basic Financial Statements – and Management's Discussion and Analysis – for State and Local Governments.* Statement 34 is arguably the most significant change in the history of governmental accounting. It is a dramatic change in the way school districts report and present financial information. The new reporting model affects every public school organization that issues financial statements in conformity with generally accepted accounting principles (GAAP).

The term reporting model is used in this publication to describe the minimum set of financial statements, note disclosures, and required supplementary information (RSI) that must be presented in a financial report for an independent auditor to assert, without qualification or further comment, that a government's financial statements are fairly presented in conformity with GAAP. The financial statements and the accompanying notes are the focus of the independent audit. However, the independent auditor is required to perform certain limited procedures in connection with RSI, such as making inquiries of management regarding RSI measurement and presentation. Notwithstanding, RSI is unaudited information.

The current financial reporting model for school districts has existed for most of the last 20 years. The National Council on Governmental Accounting (NCGA) provided a definitive form to the model with the publication of NCGA Statement 1, *Governmental Accounting and Financial Reporting Principles,* in 1979. Statement 1 contributed significantly to the standardization and enhancement of accounting and financial reporting. However, during the past several years, there has been an emerging consensus regarding the need for public schools to institute financial reporting that promotes improved fiscal and operational accountability. This consensus stimulated GASB to commence a comprehensive evaluation of the traditional financial reporting model. This effort eventually resulted in Statement 34 and the establishment of a new governmental financial reporting model.

There are two separate and equally important aspects of accountability. The understanding of these two components is critical to understanding the rationale for the enhancements provided in Statement 34. First, fiscal accountability requires that districts demonstrate compliance with public decisions concerning the raising and spending of public monies in the short term, which is usually a single budgetary cycle, or one year. Second, operational accountability requires that a district demonstrate the extent to which it has met and can continue to meet its operating objectives in an efficient and effective manner into the future.

The traditional financial reporting model has a strong emphasis on legal compliance as a means to promote fiscal accountability with only minor attention to operational accountability. Statement 34 will improve operational accountability by highlighting the district-wide perspective that was frequently lost in the detail of fund accounting. Illustration 1 presents a summary comparison of the key improvements in fiscal and operational accountability of the new governmental financial reporting model.

*Illustration 1*

***Key Changes to Fiscal and Operational Accountability***

| Changes to Enhance Financial Accountability | | Changes to Enhance Operational Accountability | |
|---|---|---|---|
| **Previous Model** | **New Model** | Previous Model | **New Model** |
| Information in basic financial statements aggregated by fund type | Information in basic financial statements presented separately for major governmental and enterprise funds | All reporting based on fund and fund types | Introduction of district-wide finanacial statements |
| Budgetary comparisons associated with the basic financial statements aggregated by fund type | Budgetary comparisons associated with the basic finanacial statements presented for the general fund and each major special revenue fund with a legally adopted annual budget | Information on governmental activities limited to near-term inflows and outflows of spendable resources | District-wide financial statements provide additional long-term focus for governmental activities |
| Budgetary comparisons report only final amended budget | Budgetary comparisons report both original and final amended budgets | Cost data available for business-type activities | Cost data provided for both governmental and business-type activities |
| | | No narrative required | Narrative overview and analysis required in the form of Management's Discussion and Analysis |

Although Statement 34 includes significant requirements that enhance financial reporting, it does not abandon the traditional public-sector approach to accounting and fiscal disclosure. Rather, GASB has integrated many of the most popular features of traditional financial reporting into the new model.

The requirements in Statement 34 are also designed to make annual reports easier for the public to understand and more useful to stakeholders, such as investors and creditors. The new standards represent a substantial advance in the disclosure of more meaningful and useful financial information by school districts.

Specifically, Statement 34 establishes new requirements for school districts' annual financial report. Illustration 2 provides the basic framework of the new model for the presentation of the annual financial report. The most important features of the model are:

***Illustration 2***
***New Financial Reporting Model: Minimum Information Required for Fair Presentation in Conformity with Generally Accepted Accounting Principals (GAAP)***

**Required Supplemental Information**
Management's Discussion and Analysis

**Basic Financial Statements**

**District-wide Financial Statements**
Statement of Net Assets
Statement of Activities

**Fund Financial Statements**
<u>Governmental Funds:</u>
Balance Sheet
Statement of Revenues, Expenditures and Changes in Fund Balances
<u>Proprietary Funds:</u>
Statement of Net Assets
Statement of Revenues, Expenses and Changes in Net Assets
Statement of Cash Flows
<u>Fiduciary Funds:</u>
Statement of Fiduciary Net Assets
Statement of Changes in Fiduciary Net Assets (not applicable to agency funds)

**Notes to the Financial Statements**

**<u>Required Supplementary Information</u>**
Budgetary Comparison Schedules
Notes to the Budgetary Comparison Schedule
Infrastructure assets reported using the modified approach (if any)
Pension Information (in certain situations)

- *Government-wide financial reporting* – Districts will be required to produce financial reports that provide a clear picture of the organization as a single, unified entity. These new "district-wide" financial statements complement rather than replace traditional fund-based financial statements. (Government-wide statements will be referred to as district-wide statements throughout this manual.)
- *Additional long-term focus for school activities* – Traditional reporting for tax-supported activities has focused on short-term inflows, outflows, and balances of available financial resources. The new financial reporting model retains this short-term focus in the governmental fund financial statements while providing a long-term perspective for these same activities in the district-wide financial statements.
- *Narrative overview and analysis* – The new model provides financial report users with a

simple narrative introduction, overview, and analysis of the basic financial statements in the form of management's discussion and analysis (MD&A).

• *Information on major funds* – There is a general consensus that fund information is most useful when presented for individual funds rather than when funds are combined, such as the aggregation of special revenue funds. Accordingly, the new financial reporting model requires the presentation of individual fund data for each of the district's major funds as defined by Statement 34.

• *Expanded budgetary reporting* – In the past, budgetary comparisons were based solely on the final amended budget. Under the new model, information on the original budget must also be presented. In addition, the new model eliminates aggregated budget presentations in favor of comparisons for the general fund and each major special revenue fund with an annual legally adopted budget.

Statement 34 is primarily based on GASB Concepts Statement No. 1, Objectives of Financial Reporting, published in 1987. Some of the objectives in Statement No. 1 affirmed the importance of the financial information that districts currently include in their annual reports. In addition, Statement No. 1 advocated new standards for financial reporting that move districts closer to the accounting standards for private-sector businesses. Statement 34 meets the Statement No. 1 objectives by requiring districts to retain much of the current information in their annual reports, in addition to the presentation of new and different financial data.
Among the major innovations of Statement 34, districts will be required to:

• Provide information about the cost of delivering services to students.

• Include, for the first time, information about general infrastructure assets of the school district, if any.

To help school business officials implement the changes in Statement 34, the Association of School Business Officials (ASBO) International has published these implementation recommendations. The Accounting, Auditing, and Budgeting Committee: Subcommittee on GASB Statement 34 Implementation prepared these recommendations.

This document presents the new standards and provides examples of the required financial reports. It is supplemented with information in two appendices. The first appendix is the illustrative MD&A provided by GASB in its school district user guide. The second appendix discusses the impact of Statement 34 on the preparation of a comprehensive annual financial report (CAFR) based on the requirements of ASBO International's Certificate of Excellence (COE).

This introduction provides a brief review of GASB, summarizes the implementation schedule for the new reporting standards, and presents an overview of the chapters to follow.

## Governmental Accounting Standards Board

GASB was formed in 1984 to develop and improve financial reporting rules for the more than 84,000 state and local governments in the United States, including school districts. It operates under the auspices of the not-for-profit Financial Accounting Foundation, which oversees and appoints the GASB members, as well as the Financial Accounting Standards Board (FASB). GASB is not part of any government. Adhering to its pronouncements is required in most states. GASB pronouncements must be followed when a state or local government's audit report states that it follows GAAP. Bond covenants associated with the issuance of debt often require school districts to follow GAAP.

## Implementation of Statement 34

School districts must prepare financial statements in accordance with the new standards in three phases, depending on the total revenues of the district in its first fiscal year ending after June 15, 1999. *Phase One* school districts with annual revenues of $100 million or more must comply with Statement 34 for fiscal years beginning after June 15, 2001. *Phase Two* school districts, with annual revenues of $10 million or more and less than $100 million, must comply for fiscal years beginning after June 15, 2002. *Phase Three* school districts, with annual revenues under $10 million, must comply for fiscal years beginning after June 15, 2003. Illustration 3 provides more detail on the implementation schedule.

***Illustration 3***
***Timetable for Implementing the New Financial Reporting Model***

| Size of Government | All provisions except retroactive reporting of major general infrastructure assets (if any) | Retroactive reporting of major general infrastructure assets |
|---|---|---|
| $100 million or more total revenues | Years beginning after 06-15-01** | Years beginning after 06-15-05 |
| Less than $100 million but ≥ $10million total annual revenues* | Years beginning after 06-15-02** | Years beginning after 06-15-06 |
| Less than $10 million total annual revenues* | Years beginning after 06-15-03** | Optional |

**For this purpose, "total revenues" are those of the school district's governmental and enterprise funds in the first fiscal year ending after June 15, 1999, excluding extraordinary items.*
***GASB 34 paragraph 142 requires component units to early implement if the primary government chooses early implementation. Accordingly, school districts that are component units must monitor the primary government's implementation timeline in order to comply with GASB 34.*

## Statement 34 Implementation Recommendations

This document is divided into six chapters addressing Statement 34 implementation recommendations. Many of the financial illustrations and statements in this guide have been adapted from the school district user guide (at this time untitled) to be published by GASB. In addition, GASB has published an implementation guide titled *"Guide to Implementation of GASB Statement 34 on Basic Financial Statements – and Management's Discussion and Analysis – for State and Local Governments."* GASB's implementation guide is presented in a question-and-answer format. Both of the GASB publications are useful resources for business officials to utilize when preparing financial statements in conformance with the new reporting model.

ASBO's implementation recommendations are specific to school districts while the GASB implementation guide is for all types of state and local governments. **ASBO's implementation recommendations are cross referenced to specific questions in GASB's implementation guide. The references are enclosed within parenthesis throughout the text. For example, (Q105-106) refers the reader to questions and answers 105 and 106 in GASB's implementation guide.** ASBO's implementation recommendations include specific guidance to meeting the requirements of Statement 34, where GASB has allowed multiple methods. ASBO believes school districts will achieve greater comparability and uniformity in financial reporting if districts apply the new standards using the same methodology.

Following is a summary of each chapter's contents.

***Management's Discussion & Analysis (Chapter One)***

School districts must include a Management's Discussion and Analysis (MD&A), which is required supplementary information (RSI). The MD&A is required to precede the basic financial statements and notes. The MD&A is intended to be an easily readable and objective analysis of the school district's financial activities. It will introduce the financial statements and provide the reader with an analysis of the district's financial activities.

The MD&A will provide an analysis of the school district's overall financial position and operating results. Its purpose is to help financial statement users assess if the district's financial position has improved or deteriorated. The analysis must include a comparison of the current year to the prior year based on the district-wide financial information about assets, liabilities, revenues, and expenses. In addition, the analysis will explain significant variations in fund-based financial results and budgetary information and will describe capital asset and long-term debt activity during the year. The MD&A will include a description of currently known facts, decisions, or conditions expected to have a significant effect on the future financial position and results of operations of the school district.

***District-wide Financial Statements (Chapter Two)***

The new basic financial statements will be composed of district-wide financial statements, fund financial statements, and notes to the financial statements. Perhaps the most notable feature of the new model is the requirement for district-wide financial statements. The focus is on the school district as a whole rather than on individual funds. The district-wide statements must be prepared on an accrual basis of accounting for all of the activities of the district. Under the accrual basis, all revenues and costs of providing services are reported, not just those received or paid in the current year or soon thereafter. This approach moves governmental accounting closer to financial reporting in the private sector.

The district-wide financial statements must be prepared on an economic resources measurement focus, which includes all of a school district's resources, both capital and financial, current and long term. The statements would therefore include current assets, capital assets, current liabilities, and long-term liabilities. The district-wide financial statements consist of two statements:

- A statement of net assets (equivalent to a balance sheet): The statement of net assets is used to report all that a school district owns (assets) and owes (liabilities). A school district's assets include financial resources such as cash, receivables, and investments. Capital assets, such as equipment, land, and buildings, are included in the statement. Liabilities include amounts owed to vendors (payables) and various debt instruments such as bonds, notes and leases as well as obligations incurred in connection with district operations such as salaries payable, unused vacation leave, claims, and judgments.

- A statement of activities (equivalent to an income statement): The statement of activities is used to report all changes in a district's net assets. This statement focuses on expenses (costs) rather than expenditures (near-term outflows of spendable resources). Expenses include depreciation on capital assets.

Each of the district-wide statements must distinguish between governmental and business-type activities of the primary government and its discretely presented component units by reporting each in separate columns. Fiduciary activities, whose resources are not available to finance school programs, are excluded from the district-wide statements.

### *Fund Financial Statements (Chapter Three)*

Until now, annual reports have divided financial information among a variety of funds. These funds have been established by governing bodies such as federal and state departments of education, state legislatures, or school districts. Such an approach facilitated the control of resources and permitted measurement, in the short term, of the revenues and expenditures arising from a particular activity. Because the users of financial information continue to assess compliance with finance-related laws, rules, and regulations, Statement 34 requires districts to continue to present financial statements with information about funds.

The focus of these fund-based statements has been sharpened, however, by requiring districts to report information about their most important or *major* funds, including the school district's "general fund." Until now, fund information has been reported in the aggregate by type of fund, which obscures individual funds. This often makes it difficult to assess a district's accountability for a significant individual program or particular dedicated revenue.

Another important objective of annual reports is to provide a comparison of the inflows of the resources of a district with its outflows. Statements for governmental funds will continue to use the flow of current financial resources measurement focus. These statements will show the short-term performance of individual funds using the same measures most districts use to manage their resources. This is in contrast to the long-term focus of accrual-based district-wide statements.

Districts will continue to provide budgetary comparison information in their annual reports. An important change, however, is a requirement to add the district's original budget to the current comparison of final budget-to-actual results. Many school districts revise their original budgets over the course of the year for a variety of reasons. The reporting of the original budget adds a new analytical dimension and increases the usefulness of the budgetary comparison. It will facilitate some assessment on how accurately a district can estimate and manage its general resources.

### *Capital Assets and Depreciation (Chapter Four)*

Statement 34 requires capitalization and depreciation of all exhaustible capital assets, including infrastructure (if any) assets, in the district-wide financial statements. Capital assets (equipment, land, and buildings) are less easily converted to cash and less spendable than financial assets (cash, receivables, and investments). Infrastructure assets, such as roads and bridges, are long-lived capital assets that are normally stationary in nature and normally can be preserved for a significantly greater number of years than most capital assets. Most school districts will not have infrastructure assets. All school districts must now capitalize and depreciate exhaustible capital assets. School districts that have infrastructure assets should refer to the GASB implementation guide for assistance in meeting reporting requirements.

### *Notes to the Financial Statements (Chapter Five)*

The notes to the financial statements provide additional information that is essential for the statements to fairly represent the school district's financial position. The notes contain important information that is not part of the financial statements. However, the notes are an integral part of the statements not an appendage to them. Statement 34 requires changes to disclosures in the notes to the financial statements for summary of significant accounting policies, capital assets, and long-term debt. Further, the notes to the financial statements may include certain detail disclosure to reconcile the differences between district-wide and fund financial statements.

### *The Comprehensive Annual Financial Report (Chapter Six)*

Many districts publish their annual financial reports as part of a larger comprehensive annual financial report (CAFR). The CAFR contains additional financial, economic, and demographic information that is useful in the analysis of the school district's financial position and operational results.

Statement 34 does not change the CAFR's basic framework, which includes an introductory section, a financial section, and a statistical section. However, the financial section must now include the MD&A, basic financial statements and other RSI as well as combining and individual nonmajor fund statements and schedules.

# Chapter One
# Management's Discussion and Analysis

This chapter provides guidance and suggestions for Management's Discussion and Analysis (MD&A), a new requirement of the reporting model. The MD&A is intended to give the reader an easy-to-understand overview of the school district's financial position and results of operations for the year. Management is required to explain the district's financial position and should include the reasons the position is improved, deteriorated, or the same when compared with the prior year. The analysis is to be based only on *currently* known facts as of the date of the auditor's report. Discussion of anticipated future developments or events is not permitted in the MD&A. The MD&A precedes and introduces the financial statements.

If the school district prepares a comprehensive annual financial report (CAFR), the MD&A does not replace the transmittal letter. The transmittal letter will still introduce the CAFR and as such will precede the MD&A (Q6). The transmittal letter should not replicate information contained in the MD&A. The transmittal letter may discuss anticipated events, which are specifically excluded from the MD&A. For more information as to the affects of Statement 34 on the CAFR, refer to Chapter Six of this guide.

MD&A is required supplementary information (RSI). As such, the auditor must give the MD&A appropriate consideration. The auditor must perform certain limited procedures and will report any deficiencies or omission.

MD&A analyses are to be made by using information contained in the new district-wide financial statements. The focus should be directed on the school district as a whole and would not emphasize component units. This assumes that the effect of the component units is not significant. If this is not the case, the extent of discussion is left to management's professional judgment and depends on the significance of the component unit(s) compared with total operations of the school district. Generally, most school district component units activity is not significant.

Statement 34, paragraphs 6a and 8 through 11, includes the specific elements of MD&A (Q10). The information that follows is a summary of those elements with suggestions and examples.

1. Although MD&A is RSI, it is required to precede the basic financial statements. It is designed to give the reader an objective and easily readable analysis of the school district's overall financial activities.

2. MD&A is management's responsibility. The analysis and associated information and conclusions are to be based on known developments and occurrences as of the date of the auditor's report. "What if" or information about potential developments or future planned events is not considered to be currently known facts and should not be included in the MD&A.

3. MD&A should emphasize current-year results in comparison with the prior year. NOTE: prior-year data is not required, but is encouraged, in the year of implementation. However, a statement to the effect that prior-year data is not available but will be provided in subsequent years must be included in the MD&A in the first year of implementation.

4. Districts are encouraged to include charts, graphs, and tables to enhance readers' understanding. Today's presentation methods are significantly improved and provide business officials with many options to develop and use tools that can enhance the readers' understanding. ASBO encourages creative development of this section and, if possible, the use of color graphics.

5. Discussion and analysis should focus on the primary government. The focus is to report the change in the school district's overall financial condition from the prior year to the current year.

6. The MD&A will introduce the new district-wide financial statements and explain the purpose and differences of both the fund financial statements and the new statements. The MD&A should help the reader understand the differences and how the statements complement each other. The narrative should describe the measurement focus and bases of accounting of both sets of financial statements (Q11).

7. The school district should explain that the district-wide financial statements are new and have not been required or provided in the past. The school district should provide a description of the two new statements, the statement of net assets and the statement of activities, and what they are intended to report. The MD&A should inform the reader that the district-wide statements encompass all assets and liabilities using the accrual basis of accounting.

8. School districts are required to analyze data reported in the financial statements and give appropriate explanations for significant changes that took place during the period.

9. Condensed financial information, derived from district-wide statements, with explanations of significant changes between the current and prior year is required. The MD&A will include information needed to support analysis of financial position and results of operation. The following elements, at a minimum, should be included in condensed information (Q12):

a. Total assets, distinguishing between capital and other assets
b. Total liabilities, distinguishing between long-term liabilities and other liabilities
c. Total net assets, distinguishing among amounts invested in capital assets, net of related debt; restricted amounts; and unrestricted amounts
d. Program revenues by major source
e. General revenues by major source
f. Total revenues
g. Program expenses, at a minimum by function
h. Total expenses
i. Excess (deficiency) before contributions to term and permanent endowments or permanent fund principal, special and extraordinary items, and transfers
j. Contributions
k. Special and extraordinary items
l. Transfers
m. Change in net assets
n. Ending net assets

10. The analysis of financial position and results of operations should help the user answer the questions listed below. The analysis should be factual, reliable, and understandable.

- Did the school district's overall financial position improve or decline from the prior year?
- Did the school district earn enough revenues during the year to cover expenses incurred during the year (did revenues equal or exceed expenses)?
- Did the school district report what it cost for services delivered?
- Did the school district generate a portion of service costs by user fees, grants, etc., or were tax revenues used to cover the cost of services?
- Did the school district's investment in capital assets change?

Figure 1.1, following, is an example of a condensed statement of net assets for a school district. It provides a summary of the school district's net assets for the fiscal year ending in 2001 compared with 2002. The accompanying analysis explains the significant changes, such as growth in current assets, the change in capital assets, why liabilities varied from one year to the next, and the change in restricted assets.

***Figure 1-1***
***Condensed Statement of Net Assets (in millions of dollars)***

| | Governmental Activities | | Business-type Activities | | Total School District | | Total Percentage Change |
|---|---|---|---|---|---|---|---|
| | 2001 | 2002 | 2001 | 2002 | 2001 | 2002 | 2001-2002 |
| Current and other assets | $117.8 | $142.8 | $ 9.9 | $ 11.2 | $ 127.7 | $ 154.0 | 20.6% |
| Net capital assets | 329.1 | 315.5 | 1.9 | 2.5 | 331.0 | 318.1 | -3.9% |
| Total assets | 446.9 | 458.4 | 11.8 | 13.7 | 458.7 | 472.1 | 2.9% |
| Long-term debt outstand | 134.0 | 118.8 | - | - | 134.0 | 118.8 | -11.3% |
| Other liabilities | 40.4 | 48.0 | 0.7 | 1.3 | 41.1 | 49.3 | 20.0% |
| Total liabilities | 174.4 | 166.8 | 0.7 | 1.3 | 175.1 | 168.1 | -4.0% |
| Net assets | | | | | | | |
| Invested in capital assets, net of related debt | 219.2 | 231.1 | 1.9 | 2.5 | 221.1 | 233.7 | 5.7% |
| Restricted | 6.0 | 5.5 | - | - | 6.0 | 5.5 | -7.5% |
| Unrestricted | 47.3 | 54.9 | 9.2 | 9.9 | 56.6 | 64.8 | 14.5% |
| Total net assets | $272.5 | $291.6 | $11.1 | $ 12.4 | $ 283.6 | $ 304.0 | 7.2% |

Note: totals may not add due to rounding.

Figure 1.2 illustrates the impact that results of operations had on changes in net assets in the fiscal year ending in 2002. This report helps the reader understand the impact revenues and expenses have on the district's overall financial position. Like the table above, the analysis should include an explanation of significant changes.

***Figure 1-2***
***Changes in Net Assets from Operating Results (in millions of dollars)***

| | Governmental Activities | | Business-type Activities | | Total School District | | Total Percentage Change |
|---|---|---|---|---|---|---|---|
| | 2001 | 2002 | 2001 | 2002 | 2001 | 2002 | 2001-2002 |
| **Revenues** | | | | | | | |
| Program revenues | | | | | | | |
| Charges for services | $ 7.9 | $ 8.5 | $5.0 | $5.7 | $12.9 | $14.2 | 10.2% |
| Operating Grants & Contributions | 38.3 | 42.3 | 15.3 | 17.0 | 53.7 | 59.3 | 10.4% |
| Capital Grants & Contributions | | | | 0.7 | - | 0.7 | |
| General revenues | | | | | | | |
| Property taxes | 162.8 | 171.0 | - | - | 162.8 | 171.0 | 5.0% |
| State formula aid | 175.0 | 176.3 | - | - | 175.0 | 176.3 | 0.7% |
| Other | 6.8 | 7.4 | 0.3 | 0.3 | 7.0 | 7.7 | 9.5% |
| **Total revenues** | **390.8** | **405.4** | **20.6** | **23.7** | **411.4** | **429.1** | **4.3%** |
| **Expenses** | | | | | | | |
| Instruction | 228.9 | 234.8 | | | 228.9 | 234.8 | 2.6% |
| Pupil & Instructional Services | 44.8 | 44.0 | | | 44.8 | 44.0 | -1.8% |
| Administration & Business | 43.7 | 41.4 | | | 43.7 | 41.4 | -5.3% |
| Maintenance & operations | 29.5 | 30.4 | | | 29.5 | 30.4 | 3.1% |
| Transportation | 8.8 | 8.6 | | | 8.8 | 8.6 | -2.3% |
| Other | 23.4 | 28.5 | 20.2 | 22.4 | 43.6 | 50.9 | 16.7% |
| **Total expenses** | **379.1** | **387.7** | **20.2** | **22.4** | **399.3** | **410.1** | **2.7%** |
| Excess (deficiency) before special item | 11.7 | 17.7 | 0.4 | 1.3 | 12.1 | 19.0 | 56.9% |
| Special item: land sale | - | 1.4 | - | - | - | 1.4 | - |
| **Increase (decrease) in net assets** | **$11.7** | **$ 19.1** | **$0.4** | **$1.3** | **$12.1** | **$20.4** | **68.2%** |

*Note: totals may not add due to rounding.*

Figure 1.3 is an example of a condensed statement showing the net cost of governmental activities. (This table exceeds GASB's minimum requirement; however, ASBO recommends including a similar table.) This table shows the district's total cost for providing the identified services. The net cost of services is the result after subtracting grants and charges for services that the district used to offset the program's total cost.

***Figure 1-3***
***Net Cost of Governmental Activities (in millions of dollars)***

| | Total Cost of Services | | Percentage Change | Net Cost of Services | | Percentage Change |
|---|---|---|---|---|---|---|
| | 2001 | 2002 | 2001-2002 | 2001 | 2002 | 2001-2002 |
| Instruction | $228.9 | $ 234.8 | 2.6% | $197.3 | $ 201.6 | 2.2% |
| Pupil & Instructional Services | $ 44.8 | $ 44.0 | -1.8% | 36.3 | 36.1 | -0.6% |
| Administration & Business | $ 43.7 | $ 41.4 | -5.3% | 39.2 | 36.8 | -6.1% |
| Maintenance & operations | $ 29.5 | $ 30.4 | 3.1% | 26.7 | 27.5 | 3.0% |
| Transportation | $ 8.8 | $ 8.6 | -2.3% | 7.6 | 7.8 | 2.6% |
| Other | $ 23.4 | $ 28.5 | 21.8% | 25.7 | 27.1 | 5.4% |
| Total | $379.1 | $ 387.7 | 2.3% | $332.8 | $ 336.9 | 1.2% |

*Note: totals may not add due to rounding.*

11. The MD&A should include an analysis of balances and transactions of individual funds. The analysis needs to identify reasons for significant changes in fund balances or fund net assets and explain any restrictions, commitments, or other limitations affecting fund resources availability for future uses.

- Management should discuss the change in fund balance(s) from the prior year for the district's major funds. Management is required to explain the reason(s) for any significant changes. An overview of changes in revenues and expenditures is appropriate. This would include an explanation of both financial (reasons for major revenue adjustments and program expenditure adjustments) and non-financial (board/district philosophy or legislative changes that affected fund balances) changes. The reasons and explanation for changes would be based on the individual circumstances of the district.

- Additional discussion is required to inform the reader of any commitments or obligations that have been placed on fund resources that limits their use in the future.

12. A condensed statement of net assets for governmental activities is illustrated in Figure 1.1. Total net assets will most likely differ from total fund balance. Therefore, a condensed reconciliation between total governmental fund balance and net assets of governmental activities may be appropriate in the MD&A to aid in further understanding the changes that have taken place.

13. All school districts are required to include budgetary comparison schedules or statements either as RSI or as part of the basic financial statements. The school district should include in the MD&A an explanation of significant differences shown in the schedule or statement. The explanation(s) should be specific to the events that took place. The district should disclose its practice/requirement for "amending" the original budget. ASBO encourages man-

agement to discuss ending results that were unanticipated, such as higher/lower cost of opening/expanding/closing facilities, change in student count/growth, program changes, change in staff or staffing patterns, revenue flow, etc.

14. The MD&A should include a description of significant capital asset and long-term debt activity that occurred during the year. The discussion needs to reveal commitments for capital expenditures, changes in credit rating, and debt limitations that may affect financing of planned facilities or services. Again, this discussion should be limited to events that have taken place, not anticipated future events.

- The notes to the financial statements require certain disclosure for capital assets and long-term liabilities. The requirement for the MD&A is to summarize the information and give additional information to explain the difference between years. Additionally, it would be appropriate to include data on legal margin of indebtedness.
- Figure 1.4, Capital Assets, illustrates changes, net of depreciation, by asset type. Management would need to explain the reason(s) for significant changes.

***Figure 1-4***
***Capital Assets (net of depreciation, in millions of dollars)***

| | Governmental Activities | | Business-type Activities | | Total School District | | Total Percentage Change |
|---|---|---|---|---|---|---|---|
| | 2001 | 2002 | 2001 | 2002 | 2001 | 2002 | 2001-2002 |
| Land | $ 22.1 | $ 20.8 | - | - | $ 22.1 | $ 20.8 | -5.6% |
| Construction in progress | 11.4 | 11.4 | - | - | 11.4 | 11.4 | 0.4% |
| Buildings | 188.5 | 177.9 | - | - | 188.5 | 177.9 | -5.7% |
| Equipment & furniture | 106.9 | 105.4 | $1.9 | $2.5 | 108.8 | 107.9 | -0.9% |
| **Total** | **$ 329.0** | **$315.5** | **$1.9** | **$2.5** | **$330.9** | **$ 318.1** | **-3.9%** |

*Note: totals may not add due to rounding.*

- Figure 1.5 illustrates a condensed summary of outstanding long-term debt, including percentage change. Management should explain the reason(s) for such changes.

***Figure 1- 5***
***Outstanding Long-Term Debt (in millions of dollars)***

| | Total School District | | Total Percentage Change |
|---|---|---|---|
| | 2001 | 2002 | 2001-2002 |
| General obligation bonds & notes (financed with property taxes) | $ 108.2 | $ 96.5 | -10.8% |
| Other general obligation debt | 5.8 | 4.7 | -19.0% |
| **Total** | $ 114.0 | $101.2 | -11.2% |

15. Statement 34 requires districts that use the modified approach to report some or all of its infrastructure assets to discuss significant changes in assessed condition, how the current assessed condition compares with the condition level the district has established, and any significant differences from the estimated annual amount to maintain or preserve infrastructure assets compared with actual amounts spent during the current year. Infrastructure (roads, bridges, water and sewer systems, etc.) is generally not an issue for school districts. Consequently this document does not provide additional information.

16. In addition to specific required information, the MD&A should include any other currently known facts that are expected to have a significant effect on the district's financial position or results of operation. It is management's responsibility to identify these changes and inform the readers so they may be aware of the potential impact to the district. For MD&A purposes, currently known facts are as of the date of the auditor's report (Q13-14). Examples include:

- changes in legislation regarding school finance
- approved capital projects
- major commercial development expected to affect the tax base
- major residential development expected to affect student enrollment
- litigation that has been concluded
- approved debt that has not had an impact, as of yet, on the school district's overall financial condition

# Chapter Two
# District-wide Financial Statements

Statement 34 requires the preparation of *district-wide* financial statements as an element of the basic financial statements (Q4). School districts must present a statement of net assets and a statement of activities. The district-wide statements present aggregated financial information using the accrual basis of accounting. Fiduciary funds are not included in this aggregated format.

Statement 34 allows a great deal of flexibility as to presentation of the new statements, particularly with regard to level of detail in reporting, function versus program reporting, allocation of depreciation and indirect expenses, and prior-year data comparison (Q15). ASBO believes that much of the new statements' benefits would be lost in the absence of some uniformity. This chapter provides an explanation of the major concepts of the new statements and implementation recommendations that will result in enhanced financial statement/reporting comparability among school districts.

This document includes sample statements and illustrations developed by ASBO's committee. ASBO encourages the use of the formats provided. However, in the event that the district does not have an amount to report under a caption, then the caption should be removed rather than reported as "zero."

## Governmental versus Business-type Activities

The district-wide presentation distinguishes between "Governmental Activities" and "Business-type Activities." The distinction between these two categories is found in Statement 34, paragraph 15, which says, in part:

"Governmental activities generally are financed through taxes, intergovernmental revenues, and other non-exchange revenues. These activities are usually reported in governmental funds and internal service funds. Business-type activities are financed in whole or in part by fees charged to external parties for goods or services. These activities are usually reported in enterprise funds."

The most common school district activity that may be classified as a business-type activity is the food service operation. Statement 34, paragraph 67, identifies the criteria that would necessitate the classification of such operations as business-type activities. In summary, if the activity is financed with debt that is secured solely by a pledge of the net revenues and fees and charges of the activity, or the laws and regulations require that costs be recovered by revenues of the activity, or the pricing policies of the activity are designed to fully recover all costs, then the activity should be classified as a business-type activity.

## Component Units

The district-wide presentation requires that discretely presented component units (as opposed to blended component units) be presented in a column immediately to the right of the column that totals the district's governmental and business-type activities (Q17). A component unit is a legally separate entity for which the district is financially accountable. It is rare for a school district to have component units. Examples could include a building project commission, a charter school, or an education foundation. GASB may address treatment of education foundations in the future. Because so few districts actually have entities that meet the requirements for classification as a component unit, this document will not address it in further detail.

## Statement of Net Assets

The Statement of Net Assets is conceptually most closely related to a balance sheet in that it reports assets, liabilities, and the difference between them. It utilizes the accounting equation: assets minus liabilities equals net assets. The statement distinguishes between the district's governmental and business-type activities. If the district has a discretely presented component unit, there should be a separate column for reporting its assets and liabilities. The illustrative statement of net assets (Figure 2-1) does not present a column for a component unit.

### *Asset Presentation*

The sample statement (Figure 2-1) is prepared in a classified format, which categorizes assets and liabilities as *current* and *non-current*. Use of the classified format is not required. An alternate format is to present assets and liabilities in order of their relative *liquidity* or *maturity*, respectively. Assets most easily convertible to cash or consumed most quickly would be presented first. GASB prefers (but does not require) the liquidity presentation at the district-wide level but requires the classified presentation for proprietary statements at the fund level (Q81). ***ASBO recommends use of the classified format presentation for the statement of net assets.*** It is ASBO's belief that consistency in presentation between the fund and district-wide presentations outweighs any advantages that may exist in presenting the liquidity format at the district-wide level.

### *Capital Assets (Q25-29)*

The most significant assets for most districts are their capital assets, such as land, buildings, and equipment. Some assets, such as land, that are inexhaustible and therefore are not depreciable, are reported in the statement of net assets at their historic cost or fair value at date of donation. Other assets, such as buildings and equipment, are exhaustible and therefore depreciable. The original or estimated historical cost of depreciable capital assets is also reported on the statement, net of accumulated depreciation. More detailed information about major classes of capital assets is presented in the notes to the financial statements. Details from this note may be presented on the statement; however, that is not required, and ASBO believes that it would clutter the face of the statement.

### *Liability Presentation*

Using the classified format, liabilities are distinguished between current and non-current. Under the liquidity format, liabilities are listed in order of how quickly they must be repaid, beginning with those that must be repaid earliest. Current liabilities include a variety of payables, such as amounts owed to employees and vendors. The most common long-term or non-current liabilities are amounts borrowed to construct buildings. Long-term debt payments are segregated into two parts: the portion that is due within one year and the remainder. In the classified format, the former is listed with the current liabilities and the latter with the non-current liabilities.

### *Net Assets*

At the district-wide level, net assets will be reported in three categories: capital assets net of related debt, restricted assets, and unrestricted assets (Q85). The following descriptions are in layman's terms. The actual definitions can be found in Statement 34, paragraphs 33-36.

- "Net assets invested in capital assets, net of related debt" is defined as capital assets less the outstanding debts incurred by the district to buy or construct the capital assets and less accumulated depreciation (Q88-94).

***Figure 2-1***
***Illustrative District-wide Statement of Net Assets***

**ASBO International School District**
**Statement of Net Assets**
**As of June 30, 2002**

| | Governmental Activities | Business-type Activities | Total |
|---|---|---|---|
| **Assets** | | | |
| **Current assets:** | | | |
| Cash and cash equivalents | $ 6,268,980 | $ 328,243 | $ 6,597,223 |
| Investments | 100,000,000 | 7,500,000 | 107,500,000 |
| Taxes receivable (net) | 12,182,730 | - | 12,182,730 |
| Due from other governmental units | 19,968,336 | 2,002,921 | 21,971,257 |
| Other receivables | 2,252,919 | 4,081 | 2,257,000 |
| Interfund loans | 615,597 | (615,597) | - |
| Inventory and prepaid expenses | 1,536,230 | 1,949,526 | 3,485,756 |
| Other current assets | 1,000 | - | 1,000 |
| Total current assets | 142,825,792 | 11,169,174 | 153,994,966 |
| **Noncurrent assets** | | | |
| Restricted cash and cash equivalents | - | - | - |
| Capital assets | 413,700,956 | 11,549,456 | 425,250,412 |
| Less: Accumulated depreciation | (98,176,725) | (9,016,026) | (107,192,751) |
| **Total noncurrent assets** | **315,524,231** | **2,533,430** | **318,057,661** |
| **Total assets** | **458,350,023** | **13,702,604** | **472,052,627** |
| **Liabilities** | | | |
| **Current liabilities:** | | | |
| Accounts payable and other current liabilities | 44,872,075 | 580,730 | 45,452,805 |
| Deferred revenue | 3,117,910 | 723,038 | 3,840,948 |
| Current portion of long-term obligations | 16,554,854 | - | 16,554,854 |
| **Total current liabilities** | **64,544,839** | **1,303,768** | **65,848,607** |
| **Noncurrent liabilities:** | | | |
| Noncurrent portion of long-term obligations | 102,242,026 | - | 102,242,026 |
| **Total non-current liabilities** | **102,242,026** | - | **102,242,026** |
| **Total liabilities** | **166,786,865** | **1,303,768** | **168,090,633** |
| **Net Assets** | | | |
| Invested in capital assets, net of related debt | 231,118,669 | 2,533,430 | 233,652,099 |
| Restricted for: | | | - |
| Debt service | 4,133,180 | - | 4,133,180 |
| Capital Projects | - | - | - |
| Other activities | 1,396,569 | - | 1,396,569 |
| Unrestricted | 54,914,740 | 9,865,406 | 64,780,146 |
| **Total net assets** | **$ 291,563,158** | **$ 12,398,836** | **$ 303,961,994** |

School district staff should analyze existing debt and ascertain whether it was issued in support of the purchase of capital asset(s). If so, every attempt should be made to capture its original cost and include it in the district's inventory. Debt incurred should be carefully evaluated for related assets, which should be capitalized. In addition, staff will need to establish a system of easily linking the debts to related assets so that production of the "Invested in capital assets, net of related debt" line of the Statement of Net Assets may be easily determined.

- "Restricted net assets." Net assets are considered restricted if their use is constrained to a particular purpose by statutes, rules, or other entities with authority over the district. The individual amounts restricted for various purposes are each identified by category. Restrictions may include amounts legally segregated for payment of debt, unspent amounts borrowed for capital projects, or the net assets of permanent funds.
- "Unrestricted." These are the resources that do not fall into the first two categories. They can be used for any purpose, though they are not necessarily liquid. District designations of funds for purposes such as cash flow or other activities are reported here but are not identified separately (Q101-102).

School officials should be aware of the possibility of unrestricted deficits; however, deficits for the total net assets are unlikely. In some cases, a school district may maintain an unrestricted deficit because it has not accumulated resources to offset certain long-term liabilities, such as compensated absences, claims, or judgments. ASBO encourages districts to consider the impact of reporting negative unrestricted assets (or total net assets). An aggressive capitalization policy could help to preclude this from occurring. Further, there is a possibility that other liabilities (such as other post-employment benefits) may be recognized in the future, thereby making the likelihood of negative net assets more probable.

## Statement of Activities

The Statement of Activities is conceptually most closely related to an income statement, in that it reports revenues, expenses, and other changes in net assets. It reports gross expenses, offsetting program revenues and net cost information at the function or program level for the current year. General and other revenues are reported separately from program revenues. ***Figure 2-2 represents ASBO's recommended minimum reporting format.*** The significance of this statement is that, for the first time, there is a presentation of the district's net cost, financed by general revenues, of each major activity (Q103).

### *Expenses*

The minimum requirement for presentation of expenses is by function, rather than by program. ***ASBO believes that reporting by function and remaining closely aligned with functions as distinguished in the Federal Accounting Handbook 2R2 will provide the most easily understandable statement.*** ASBO strongly encourages districts that choose to report at a level of detail greater than recommended to provide sub-totals at the same level as ASBO's recommended reporting functions. Most of the function categories are self-explanatory. However, there are a few functions that can be interpreted in a variety of ways depending upon individual state requirements. The following will be helpful in providing clarification for the following functions:

- Other instruction may include adult instruction that is not reported as part of community services, bilingual, gifted, summer school, extra and co-curricular programs, and instructional technology.

***Figure 2-2***
***Illustrative District-wide Statement of Activities***

**ASBO International School District**
**Statement of Activities**
**For the Year ended June 30, 2002**

| | | Program Revenues | | | Net (Expenses) Revenue and Changes In Net Assets | | |
|---|---|---|---|---|---|---|---|
| **Functions/Programs** | **Expenses** | **Charges for Services** | **Operating Grants and Contributions** | **Capital Grants and s** | **Government Activities** | **Business Type Activities** | **Total** |
| **Governmental activities:** | | | | | | | |
| Instruction: | | | | | | | |
| Regular instruction | $ 187,819,890 | $ 3,096,599 | $ 22,105,041 | | $ (162,618,250) | | $ (162,618,250) |
| Special education instruction | 35,216,229 | | 4,144,695 | | (31,071,534) | | (31,071,534) |
| Vocational education | 10,564,869 | 1,956,842 | 1,243,408 | | (7,364,619) | | (7,364,619) |
| Other instruction | 1,173,874 | 456,278 | 138,157 | | (579,439) | | (579,439) |
| Total Instruction | 234,774,862 | 5,509,719 | 27,631,301 | - | (201,633,842) | | (201,633,842) |
| Support services: | | | | | - | | |
| Pupil services | 37,311,861 | 2,986,172 | 4,203,974 | | (30,121,715) | | (30,121,715) |
| Instructional staff services | 8,715,981 | | 756,698 | | (7,959,283) | | (7,959,283) |
| General administration services | 9,365,149 | | 3,026,792 | | (6,338,357) | | (6,338,357) |
| School administration services | 26,863,926 | | 1,055,183 | | (25,808,743) | | (25,808,743) |
| Business services | 5,164,191 | | 491,856 | | (4,672,335) | | (4,672,335) |
| Operations & maintenance of plant services | 30,411,349 | | 2,896,485 | | (27,514,864) | | (27,514,864) |
| Pupil transportation services | 8,606,985 | | 819,759 | | (7,787,226) | | (7,787,226) |
| Central services | | | | | - | | - |
| Other support services | 13,197,377 | | 1,256,965 | | (11,940,412) | | (11,940,412) |
| Community services | 2,753,346 | | 131,297 | | (2,622,049) | | (2,622,049) |
| Interest on long-term debt | 5,969,465 | | | | (5,969,465) | | (5,969,465) |
| Depreciation - unallocated* | 6,555,053 | | | | (6,555,053) | | (6,555,053) |
| Total Support Services | 154,914,683 | 2,986,172 | 14,639,009 | - | (137,289,502) | | (137,289,502) |
| Total governmental activities | 389,689,545 | 8,495,891 | 42,270,310 | - | (338,923,344) | | (338,923,344) |
| **Business-type activities:** | | | | | | | |
| Food services | 20,596,032 | 4,750,350 | 15,849,235 | $ 750,000 | | $ 753,553 | 753,553 |
| Adult education | 1,837,753 | 936,150 | 1,102,491 | | | 200,888 | 200,888 |
| **Total business-type activities** | **22,433,785** | **5,686,500** | **16,951,726** | **750,000** | | **954,441** | **954,441** |
| **Total school district** | **$ 412,123,330** | **$ 14,182,391** | **$ 59,222,036** | **$ 750,000** | **(338,923,344)** | **954,441** | **(337,968,903)** |
| **General revenues:** | | | | | | | |
| Taxes | | | | | | | |
| Property taxes, levied for general purposes | | | | | 154,108,322 | | 154,108,322 |
| Property taxes, levied for debt services | | | | | 16,860,557 | | 16,860,557 |
| Property taxes, levied for specific purposes (list each) | | | | | | | - |
| Other taxes | | | | | | | - |
| Federal and State aid not restricted to specific purposes | | | | | | | - |
| General | | | | | 176,265,211 | | 176,265,211 |
| Other | | | | | | | - |
| Interest and investment earnings | | | | | 7,397,103 | 312,271 | 7,709,374 |
| Miscellaneous | | | | | | | - |
| **Subtotal, general revenues** | | | | | **354,631,193** | **312,271** | **354,943,464** |
| **Excess (deficiency) of revenues over expenses before special items** | | | | | **15,707,849** | **1,266,712** | **16,974,561** |
| Transfers | | | | | | | |
| Special items - gain on sale of unimproved land | | | | | 1,367,341 | | 1,367,341 |
| Extraordinary items | | | | | | | |
| **Total general revenues, transfers, special, and extraordinary items** | | | | | **355,998,534** | **312,271** | **356,310,805** |
| **Changes in net assets** | | | | | **17,075,190** | **1,266,712** | **18,341,902** |
| Net assets - beginning | | | | | 272,487,968 | 11,132,124 | 283,620,092 |
| Net assets - ending | | | | | $ 289,563,158 | $ 12,398,836 | $ 301,961,994 |

**This amount excludes the depreciation that is included in the direct expenses of the various functions. See Note 2.*

- Instructional staff services include improvement of instruction, learning media center, and student assessment and testing.
- General administration services include superintendent, board of education, and support services administration.
- Business services include fiscal services and data processing services.
- Central services include centrally provided services that are not charged back to individual functions, information services, and planning and research services.
- Depreciation (unallocated) includes the depreciation that has not been allocated to a specific expense function.

### *Depreciation*

The measurement focus and basis of accounting used in the statement of activities results in the need for depreciation of capital assets. As a result, items purchased and capitalized in the current year will not be reported as current expenses on the statement of activities. The depreciation for assets directly associated with a specific function or a small number of functions is required to be reported as a direct expense of that function(s). Consequently, staff will need to establish policies and procedures for identifying and classifying direct versus indirect assets at the time of purchase and whenever changes are made to its assignment.

Depreciation of assets that serve essentially all functions may be allocated among the functions, included in a "general" expenses function or reported as a separate cost. ***ASBO recommends reporting depreciation expense not directly related to specific functions on a separate line titled "Depreciation (unallocated)." Including depreciation expense in the general expenses function would inflate a cost that many taxpayers are already very attentive to, and ASBO is not in favor of allocated indirect expenses.***

### *Indirect Expense Allocation (Q105-106)*

GASB allows the district to include an indirect expense column to the right of the expenses column and allocate indirect expenses such as interest on long-term debt, depreciation (Q108) and general administration over the remaining functions of the district. ***ASBO discourages this approach.*** ASBO believes that some taxpayers would interpret this as an attempt to hide administrative costs among other functions. Further, there are a variety of allocation methods that districts could utilize, which would further complicate the process of achieving uniformity and comparability.

### *Program Revenues*

The columns to the right of gross expenses present the district's program revenues. These revenues are classified by the function identified to the left (Q115-116). These are of two types:

- Charges for Services (Q117-118) are fees and other charges to the users or recipients of the services the district provides. This could include items such as: food service sales and reimbursements, rental fees for school buses or facilities, athletic participant or spectator fees, tuition, or library fines.
- Grants and Contributions (Q119-121) are funds the district receives that are restricted for a particular purpose. This could include items such as title programs, special education, transportation, and food and nutrition aid. The statement separates these grants into two categories:
  - Operating – to finance the district's annual operating activities; and
  - Capital – to fund the acquisition, construction, or renovation of capital assets.

Refer to Figure 2-3 for guidance on treatment of various revenues.

***Figure 2-3 -***
***Illustrative Classification of Revenues by NCES Title***

| NCES TITLE | PROGRAM REVENUES: Charges for Services | PROGRAM REVENUES: Operating Grants and Contributions | PROGRAM REVENUES: Capital Grants and Contributions | GENERAL PURPOSE | SPECIAL/ EXTRAORDINARY ITEMS |
|---|---|---|---|---|---|
| Property Taxes | | | | Always | |
| Payments in Lieu of Taxes | | | | Always | |
| Interfund Payments | Potentially | Potentially | Potentially | Potentially | |
| Payments for Services (tuition) | Generally | | | Potentially | |
| Food Service Sales | Always | | | | |
| Non-Capital Sales | Generally | | | Potentially | |
| School Activity Income | Generally | | | Potentially | |
| Interest on Investments | Potentially | | | Generally | |
| Other Local Revenue | Potentially | | | Generally | |
| Interdistrict Transit of Aids | Potentially | Potentially | Potentially | Potentially | |
| Interdistrict Tuition Payment | Generally | | | Potentially | |
| Other Interdistrict Payments | Potentially | Potentially | Potentially | Potentially | |
| Intermediate Transit of Aids | Potentially | Potentially | Potentially | Potentially | |
| Intermediate Payment for Services | Generally | | | Potentially | |
| Other Intermediate Payments | Potentially | Potentially | Potentially | Potentially | |
| Categorical State Aid | Potentially | Potentially | Potentially | Potentially | |
| General State Aid | | | | Always | |
| State Payments for Special Projects | | Generally | Potentially | | |
| State Tuition Payments | Generally | | | Potentially | |
| State Payments through Local Units | Potentially | | | Generally | |
| Federal Categorical Aid | | Generally | Potentially | | |
| Federal Impact Aid | | | | Generally | |
| Federal Payments for Special Projects | | Generally | Potentially | | |
| Gain or loss on sale of fixed assets | | | | | Generally |
| Borrowed amounts | | | | | |
| Refund of Prior Year Disbursements | | | | Generally | |

### *Net Cost of Services*

The column titled "Net (Expenses) Revenue and Changes in Net Assets" is significant because it shows the net cost or revenue of each function of the school district. These dollar amounts are calculated by subtracting total program revenues from the expenses of each function. If the expenses of the district's functions surpass program revenues, negative numbers result in the statement, representing a net expense or net cost to the general public. These functions are generally dependent upon general-purpose revenues, including tax dollars. When program revenues exceed expenses, the resulting number is positive, representing a net revenue to the general public, sometimes available to offset other program costs. The "positive" and "negative" numbers should not be construed as value judgments. They are merely indicative of whether a particular function relies on general revenues for financing or is a net contributor of resources to the district.

### *General Revenues*

General revenues are presented immediately below the total net expense of the functions. General revenues represent the revenues available to the school district to finance the net cost of services not funded by program revenues. These revenues should be presented as follows:

The first major source is "Property Taxes," which ***ASBO recommends be segregated as follows:***

- Property taxes levied for general purposes include property taxes for education, special education, and building operations
- Property taxes levied for debt services include property taxes for bonded debt that have resulted in a property tax levy schedule
- Property taxes levied for specific purposes include property taxes for tort

immunity, transportation, fire prevention and safety, state retirement programs, and any other specifically segregated levy

• Other taxes include taxes that are not derived from the property tax levy process (e.g., sales taxes)

The second major source is federal and state aid not restricted to specific purposes. The presentation of these revenues is separated between General and Other. The remaining general revenues sources are interest and investment earnings (Q130) and miscellaneous. Refer to Figure 2-3 for guidance on treatment of various revenues.

***Transfers, Special Items, Extraordinary Items***

Immediately below the general revenues, the district reports several other transactions and financial events that affect net assets. Transfers reflect financial transactions between governmental and business-type activities that are not based on receiving anything in return. Transfers between governmental and business-type activities are reported on the district-wide statements, and transfers within governmental and business-type activities are eliminated at the district-wide statement level.

Special items and/or extraordinary items are financial events that are unusual in nature and infrequent in occurrence (Q139-142). Definitions for these items can be found in Statement 34, paragraphs 55-56. They are shown separately from revenues and expenses specifically because they are not representative of the district's usual annual financial transactions.

***Net Assets***

The beginning and ending net assets are presented to reconcile the change in net assets.

# Chapter Three
# Fund Financial Statements

This chapter describes changes related to a district's fund financial statements. (See Chapter 6 for information about combining fund financial statements and a comprehensive annual financial report (CAFR)). As described in Chapter 2, the district-wide financial statements provide an all-inclusive view. The fund financial statements provide a more detailed look at specific activities or groups of activities (Q157). The governmental fund financial statements are presented on a modified accrual basis, whereas governmental activities in the district-wide financial statements are presented on an accrual basis of accounting. The fund statements will be divided into governmental funds statements, proprietary funds statements and fiduciary funds statements.

The first significant change to the fund statements required by Statement 34 is a move from "fund-type" to "major fund" (Q175) presentation. Major fund presentation is required for governmental and enterprise funds. The school district will report each major fund in a separate column on the fund financial statements with all the non-major funds presented in a single column.

The district's most significant governmental and enterprise funds as defined by GASB 34 are considered major funds. The district's main operating fund (usually the general fund) is always reported as a major fund. Other funds are classified as major if (Q 182-188 and Appendix 4, Exercise 5):

a. Total assets, liabilities, revenues, or expenditures/expenses of that individual governmental or enterprise fund are at least 10 percent of the corresponding total (assets, liabilities, and so forth) of all funds of that category; AND
b. Total assets, liabilities, revenues, or expenditures/expenses of the individual governmental fund or enterprise fund are at least 5 percent of the total for all governmental and enterprise funds combined.

The school district may also display any other governmental or enterprise fund as a major fund if it believes that the fund is important to the users of its financial statements. This criteria gives school districts the discretion to include the same funds from year to year for consistency, even if the criteria in (a) & (b) above are not met. Business officials should consider long-term reporting implications when exercising this option.

All funds that are not reported as major are considered non-major funds (Q176). These funds are aggregated and presented in a single column for each category. The major fund concept does not apply to internal service or fiduciary funds.

Another change Statement 34 requires is dropping the concept of expendable and non-expendable trust funds. Further, fiduciary funds are defined differently. Funds previously reported as non-expendable, whose resources are used to support school district operations, are now reported in a new governmental fund type called "permanent funds." Permanent funds account for resources legally restricted such that only the earnings they generate, and not the principal, may be used to finance operations (Q159). Funds previously reported as non-expendable, whose resources are NOT used to support school district operations, will continue to be reported in a fiduciary fund.

Funds previously reported as expendable fiduciary funds and whose resources are used to support district operations, are now reported in a special revenue fund. Previous expendable funds whose resources are NOT used to support district operations are reported in an agency fund.

## Governmental Funds Statements

The governmental funds track the finances of a school district's basic services and, collectively, are virtually the same, after considering the different measurement focus and basis of accounting, as the governmental activities reported in the district-wide statements. They include the general, special revenue, debt service, capital projects, and the new permanent funds. Governmental fund statements represent a short-term financial view and tend to be focused on budgetary and/or regulatory compliance.

Figure 3-1 presents an illustration of the Governmental Funds Balance Sheet, and Figure 3-2 presents an illustration of the Governmental Funds Statement of Revenues, Expenditures, and Changes in Fund Balances. The district's major funds are presented in separate columns with all non-major funds presented in one column labeled *"Other Governmental Funds"* with all columns being totaled. If the school district wishes to present the non-major funds individually, it can do so by presenting these funds in combining financial statements (see Chapter 6).

***Figure 3-1 - Illustrative Governmental Funds Balance Sheet***

**ASBO International School District**
**Balance Sheet**
**Governmental Funds**
**As of June 30, 2002**

| | General Fund | Debt Service Fund | Other Governmental Funds | Total Governmental Funds |
|---|---|---|---|---|
| **ASSETS** | | | | |
| Cash and cash equivalents | $ 100,864,805 | $ 3,294,850 | $ 2,109,325 | $ 106,268,980 |
| Property taxes receivable | 15,179,756 | 2,702,625 | — | 17,882,381 |
| Less allowance for uncollectible taxes | (4,838,244) | (861,407) | — | (5,699,651) |
| Due from other governments | 15,105,826 | — | 4,862,510 | 19,968,336 |
| Accrued interest | 504,757 | — | — | 504,757 |
| Due from other funds | 5,170,479 | 759,359 | 1,852,454 | 7,782,292 |
| Other receivables | 1,218,640 | 20,695 | 508,827 | 1,748,162 |
| Inventories--supplies and materials | 1,412,121 | — | — | 1,412,121 |
| Other current assets | 125,109 | — | — | 125,109 |
| **Total assets** | **$134,743,249** | **$ 5,916,122** | **$ 9,333,116** | **$149,992,487** |
| **LIABILITIES AND FUND BALANCES** | | | | |
| **Liabilities:** | | | | |
| Accounts payable and accrued liabilities | $ 30,270,632 | $ 8,740 | $ 933,434 | $ 31,212,806 |
| Due to other funds | 20,845,752 | — | 5,503,492 | 26,349,244 |
| Due to other governments | 10,093 | — | — | 10,093 |
| Due to student groups | — | — | 256,183 | 256,183 |
| Deferred revenue | 12,283,000 | 1,774,202 | 1,243,438 | 15,300,640 |
| Amounts held for granting agencies | 233,035 | — | — | 233,035 |
| **Total liabilities** | **63,642,512** | **1,782,942** | **7,936,547** | **73,362,001** |
| **Fund Balances:** | | | | |
| Reserved for: | | | | |
| Inventories | 1,412,121 | — | — | 1,412,121 |
| Retirement of long-term debt | — | 4,133,180 | — | 4,133,180 |
| Encumbrances | 4,744,173 | — | — | 4,744,173 |
| Unreserved: | | | | |
| Designated | 21,347,665 | — | — | 21,347,665 |
| Undesignated, reported in: | | | | |
| General fund | 43,596,778 | — | — | 43,596,778 |
| Special revenue funds | — | — | 1,396,569 | 1,396,569 |
| **Total fund balances** | **71,100,737** | **4,133,180** | **1,396,569** | **76,630,486** |
| **Total liabilities and fund balances** | **$134,743,249** | **$ 5,916,122** | **$ 9,333,116** | **$149,992,487** |

***Figure 3-2***
***Illustrative Governmental Funds Statement of Revenues, Expenditures, and Changes in Fund Balances***

**ASBO International School District**
**Statement of Revenues, Expenditures and Changes in Fund Balance**
**Governmental Funds**
**For the Year Ended June 30, 2002**

| | General Fund | Debt Service Fund | Other Gov't Funds | Total Gov't Funds |
|---|---|---|---|---|
| **Revenues:** | | | | |
| Property Taxes | 153,862,367 | 16,589,425 | | 170,451,792 |
| Other Local Sources | 8,404,240 | 194,926 | 124,789 | 8,723,955 |
| Intermediate Sources | 2,106,451 | | 4,225,941 | 6,332,392 |
| State Sources | 188,019,530 | | 6,135,833 | 194,155,363 |
| Federal Sources | 2,284,748 | | 22,095,410 | 24,380,158 |
| Other Sources | 395,088 | | 441,559 | 836,647 |
| **TOTAL REVENUES** | **355,072,424** | **16,784,351** | **33,023,532** | **404,880,307** |
| **Expenditures:** | | | | |
| **Instruction:** | | | | |
| Regular Instruction | 146,067,673 | | 28,481 | 146,096,155 |
| Special Instruction | 33,937,539 | | 25,907,721 | 59,845,259 |
| Other Instruction | 26,953,263 | | | 26,953,263 |
| **Total Instruction** | **206,958,475** | | **25,936,202** | **232,894,677** |
| **Support Services** | | | | |
| Pupil Services | 34,010,001 | | 3,003,049 | 37,013,050 |
| Instructional Staff Services | 6,297,055 | | 1,825,705 | 8,122,760 |
| General Administration Services | 9,290,149 | | | 9,290,149 |
| School Administration Services | 25,188,224 | | | 25,188,224 |
| Business Services | 6,047,066 | | | 6,047,066 |
| Operations & Maintenance | 29,406,867 | | | 29,406,867 |
| Pupil Transportation | 8,322,698 | | 1,308,415 | 9,631,113 |
| Central Services | 0 | | | 0 |
| Community Services | 1,691,107 | | 1,040,189 | 2,731,296 |
| Principal and Interest | 1,538,918 | 15,894,705 | 504,668 | 17,938,291 |
| Other Support Services | 12,761,469 | | 8,327 | 12,769,796 |
| **Total Support Services** | **134,553,554** | **15,894,705** | **7,690,353** | **158,138,612** |
| **TOTAL EXPENDITURES** | **341,512,029** | **15,894,705** | **33,626,555** | **391,033,289** |
| **Excess (deficiency) of revenues over expenditures** | **13,560,395** | **889,646** | **(603,023)** | **13,847,018** |
| **Other Financing Sources (Uses):** | | | | |
| Proceeds from Capital Leases | | | 692,245 | 692,245 |
| **Special Items** | | | | |
| Proceeds from sale of Capital Assets | | | 2,601,908 | 2,601,908 |
| **NET CHANGE IN FUND BALANCES** | **13,560,395** | **889,646** | **2,691,130** | **17,141,171** |
| Fund Balance - Beginning | 54,938,434 | 3,243,534 | 1,307,347 | 59,489,315 |
| Fund Balance - Ending | 68,498,829 | 4,133,180 | 3,998,477 | 76,630,486 |

Since the district-wide and fund financial statements use different bases of accounting, a summary reconciliation is required. The objective of this summary reconciliation is to describe the differences between the fund and district-wide statements. Both governmental fund statements must be reconciled to the governmental activities in the district-wide statements. These reconciliations may be presented directly on the fund statements or on an accompanying, separate schedule following each fund statement. ***ASBO recommends a separate schedule for the reconciliation*** (see Figures 3-3 and 3-4). This will allow for a more complete explanation of the reconciling items and may preclude the need for additional note disclosures.

***Figure 3-3***
***Illustrative Reconciliation of Governmental Funds Balance Sheet to District Wide Statement of Net Assets (Separate Statement Option)***

**ASBO International School District**
**Reconciliation of the Governmental Funds Balance Sheet**
**with the Statement of Net Assets**
**June 30, 2002**

**Amounts reported for governmental activities in the statement of net assets are different because:**

| | | |
|---|---|---|
| **Total fund balance - governmental funds** | | **$76,630,486** |
| Capital assets used in governmental activities are not financial resources and therefore are not reported as assets in governmental funds. | | |
| The cost of capital assets is | 413,700,956 | |
| Accumulated depreciation is | 98,176,725 | |
| | | 315,524,231 |
| Property taxes receivable will be collected this year, but are not available soon enough to pay for the current period's expenditures, and therefore are deferred in the funds. | | 12,182,730 |
| An internal service fund is used by the District's management to charge the costs of the unemployment compensation insurance program to the individual funds. The assets and liabilities of the internal service fund are included with governmental activities. | | 6,022,591 |
| Long-term liabilities, including bonds payable, are not due and payable in the current period and therefore are not reported as liabilities in the funds. Long-term liabilities at year end consist of: | | |
| Bonds payable | 80,575,118 | |
| Accrued interest on the bonds | 759,880 | |
| Capital leases payable | 1,062,861 | |
| Contracts payable | 2,767,583 | |
| Compensated absences (vacations) | 1,125,503 | |
| Special termination benefits payable | 16,491,286 | |
| In addition, in 1990, the district issued "capital appreciation" bonds (for example, the price of a bond was $640, but redeemable at maturity for $1,000). The accretion of interest on those bonds to date is | 16,014,649 | (118,796,880) |
| **Total net assets--governmental activities** | | **$ 291,563,158** |

*Figure 3-4*
***Illustrative Reconciliation of Net Change in Fund Balances with Change in Net Assets (Separate Page Format)***

**ASBO International School District**
**Reconciliation of the Governmental Funds Statement of Revenues, Expenditures, and Changes in Fund Balances with the District-wide Statement of Activities**
**For the Year Ended June 30, 2002**

| | | | |
|---|---|---|---|
| **Total net change in fund balances--governmental funds** | | | **$ 17,141,171** |
| Amounts reported for governmental *activities* in the statement of activities are different because: | | | |
| Capital outlays to purchase or build capital assets are reported in governmental funds as expenditures. However, for governmental activities those costs are shown in the statement of net assets and allocated over their estimated useful lives as annual depreciation expenses in the statement of activities. This is the amount by which depreciation exceeds capital outlays in the period. | | | |
| Depreciation expense | $ | 13,108,809 | |
| Capital outlays | | (930,864) | (12,177,945) |
| Some of the capital assets acquired this year were financed with capital leases. The amount financed by the leases is reported in the governmental funds as a source of financing. On the other hand, the capital leases are not revenues in the statement of activities, but rather constitute long-term liabilities in the statement of net assets. | | | (692,245) |
| Because some property taxes will not be collected for several months after the District's fiscal year ends, they are not considered as "available" revenues in the governmental funds, and are instead counted as deferred tax revenues. They are, however, recorded as revenues in the statement of activities. | | | 517,087 |
| In the statement of activities, only the *gain* on the sale of the unimproved land is reported, whereas in the governmental funds, the entire proceeds from the sale increase financial resources. Thus, the change in net assets differs from the change in fund balances by the *cost* of the land sold. | | | (1,234,567) |
| In the statement of activities, certain operating expenses--compensated absences (vacations) and special termination benefits (early retirement)--are measured by the amounts *earned* during the year. In the governmental funds, however, expenditures for these items are measured by the amount of financial resources used (essentially, the amounts actually *paid* ). This year, special termination benefits paid ($10,300,426) *exceeded* the amounts earned ($7,906,074) by $2,394,352. Vacation used ($261,132) was *less than* the amounts earned ($327,280) by $66,148. | | | 2,328,204 |
| Repayment of bond principal is an expenditure in the governmental funds, but it reduces long-term liabilities in the statement of net assets and does not affect the statement of activities. | | | 13,526,946 |
| Interest on long-term debt in the statement of activities differs from the amount reported in the governmental funds because interest is recorded as an expenditure in the funds when it is due, and thus requires the use of current financial resources. In the statement of activities, however, interest expense is recognized as the interest accrues, regardless of when it is due. The additional interest reported in the statement of activities is the net result of two factors. First, accrued interest on bonds, leases, and contracts payable *decreased* by $43,380. Second, $1,601,500 of additional accumulated interest was accreted on the district's "capital appreciation" bonds. | | | (1,558,120) |
| An internal service fund is used by the District's management to charge the costs of the unemployment compensation insurance program to the individual funds. The net revenue of the internal service fund is reported with governmental activities. | | | 1,224,659 |
| **Change in net assets of governmental activities.** | | | **$ 19,075,190** |

The reconciliation for the balance sheet explains the differences between the total fund balance for the governmental funds statements and the total net assets reported for governmental activities on the government wide statements. The reconciliation for the statement of revenues, expenditures, and changes in fund balances explains the differences between the net change in fund balances for the combined governmental funds and changes in net assets for governmental activities. More disclosure may be provided in the notes to financial statements (see Figures 5-4 & 5-5).

The statement of revenues, expenditures, and changes in fund balances contains the same major funds as the balance sheet. Revenues are classified by source, such as local revenue, property tax, and state aid. Expenditures are presented by function, the same as in the district-wide financial statements. The inclusion of debt service and capital outlay expenditures on the statement of revenues, expenditures, and changes in fund balances is the major difference from the district-wide expenses on the statement of activities. Statement 34 eliminates the General Fixed Assets and General Long-Term Debt Account Groups. Therefore, the assets and liabilities previously reported in the account groups are now reported only in the district-wide financial statements.

## Proprietary Funds Statements

Proprietary funds are activities that a school district operates similar to a business, in that it attempts to recover costs through charges to the user. The proprietary funds have not changed under Statement 34 and include the enterprise and internal service funds. However, the definitions of those fund types did change somewhat, and the district staff should review them.

Enterprise funds may be used to account for any activity or service that charges a fee to external users to cover the cost of operations, including costs of depreciation and debt service. An enterprise must be used to report activities that meet any of the following criteria:

a. activities financed by debt that is secured solely by a pledge of the net revenues from fees and charges (i.e. revenue bonds), or

b. laws or regulations require that the activity's costs of providing services, including capital costs (such as depreciation or debt service) be recovered with fees and charges, rather than with taxes or similar revenues, or

c. the district's pricing policies establish fees and charges designed to recover its costs, including capital costs.

Internal service funds account for goods and services that are provided to other funds in return for a fee to cover the cost of operations, including depreciation and debt service costs. Internal service funds may enter into transactions with other governments, providing that the reporting district is the predominant participant in the fund's activities.

The proprietary funds statements include the statement of net assets; statement of revenues, expenses and changes in fund net assets; and a statement of cash flows prepared using the direct method. These statements use the accrual basis of accounting, similar to the district-wide statements. The statement of net assets is required to be prepared using the classified approach. Figure 3-5 illustrates the proprietary funds statement of net assets. The major enterprise funds are presented in individual columns, and all non-major enterprise funds, if any, are aggregated and reported in a single column. The internal service funds are presented in a single column to the right of the total column for enterprise funds. Figure 3-6 illustrates the statement of revenues, expenses, and changes in fund net assets. Figure 3-7 illustrates the Statement of Cash Flows.

***Figure 3-5***
***Illustrative Proprietary Funds Statement of Net Assets***

**ASBO International School District**
**Statement of Net Assets**
**Proprietary Funds**
**As of June 30, 2002**

| | Business-Type Activities: Enterprise Funds | | | Governmental Activities: Internal Service Fund |
|---|---|---|---|---|
| | Adult Education | Food Service | Total | |
| **ASSETS** | | | | |
| **Current Assets:** | | | | |
| Cash and cash equivalents | $ 1,857,211 | $ 5,971,032 | $ 7,828,243 | - |
| Due from other governments | 599,005 | 1,268,411 | 2,002,921 | - |
| Due from other funds | - | - | - | $ 17,589,312 |
| Other receivables | 35,803 | 3,783 | 4,081 | - |
| Inventories--supplies and materials | 477,150 | 1,572,376 | 1,949,526 | - |
| **Total Current Assets** | **2,969,169** | **8,815,602** | **11,784,771** | **17,589,312.00** |
| **Noncurrent Assets:** | | | | |
| Furniture and equipment (net) | - | 2,533,430 | 2,533,430 | - |
| **Total assets** | **2,969,169** | **11,349,032** | **14,318,201** | **17,589,312** |
| **LIABILITIES** | | | | |
| **Current Liabilities** | | | | |
| Accounts payable and accrued liabil | 96,579 | 484,151 | 580,730 | 11,566,721 |
| Due to other funds | 173,058 | 442,539 | 615,597 | — |
| Deferred revenue | 202,003 | 521,035 | 723,038 | — |
| **Total Liabilities** | **471,640** | **1,447,725** | **1,919,365** | **11,566,721** |
| **NET ASSETS** | | | | |
| Invested in capital assets | — | 2,533,430 | 2,533,430 | — |
| Unrestricted | 2,497,529 | 7,367,877 | 9,865,406 | 6,022,591 |
| **Total net assets** | **$ 2,497,529** | **$ 9,901,307** | **$ 12,398,836** | **$ 6,022,591** |

***Figure 3-6***
***Illustrative Proprietary Funds Statement of Revenues, Expenses, and Changes in Fund Net Assets***

**ASBO International School District**
**Statement of Revenues, Expenses, and Changes in Fund Net Assets**
**Proprietary Funds**
**For the Year Ended June 30, 2002**

| | Business-Type Activities: Enterprise Funds | | | Governmental Activities: Internal Service Fund |
|---|---|---|---|---|
| | Adult Education | Food Services | Total | |
| **Operating revenues:** | | | | |
| Local and intermediate sources | $ 936,150 | $ 4,750,350 | $ 5,686,500 | $ 23,864,586 |
| **Total operating revenues** | **936,150** | **4,750,350** | **5,686,500** | **23,864,586** |
| **Operating expenses:** | | | | |
| Payroll costs | 888,793 | 10,494,786 | 11,383,579 | — |
| Professional and contract services | — | 343,439 | 343,439 | — |
| Supplies and materials | 67,228 | 8,773,317 | 8,840,545 | — |
| Facility rental | 826,746 | — | 826,746 | — |
| Other operating costs | 54,986 | 984,490 | 1,039,476 | 22,639,927 |
| **Total operating expenses** | **1,837,753** | **20,596,032** | **22,433,785** | **22,639,927** |
| **Operating income (loss)** | **(901,603)** | **(15,845,682)** | **(16,747,285)** | **1,224,659** |
| **Nonoperating revenues (expenses):** | | | | |
| Interest income | 10,861 | 301,410 | 312,271 | — |
| Grants | 1,102,491 | 15,849,235 | 16,951,726 | — |
| **Total nonoperating revenues (expenses)** | **1,113,352** | **16,150,645** | **17,263,997** | **—** |
| **Income (loss) before capital contributions** | **211,749** | **304,963** | **516,712** | **1,224,659** |
| Capital contributions | — | 750,000 | 750,000 | — |
| Change in net assets | 211,749 | 1,054,963 | 1,266,712 | 1,224,659 |
| Total net assets--Beginning | 2,285,780 | 8,846,344 | 11,132,124 | 4,797,932 |
| Total net assets--Ending | $ 2,497,529 | $ 9,901,307 | $ 12,398,836 | $ 6,022,591 |

***Figure 3-7***
***Illustrative Proprietary Funds Statement of Cash Flows***

**ASBO International School District**
**Statement of Cash Flows**
**Proprietary Funds**
**For the Year Ended June 30, 2002**

| | Business-Type Activities: Enterprise Funds | | | Governmental Activities: |
|---|---|---|---|---|
| | **Adult Education** | **Food Services** | **Total** | **Internal Service Fund** |
| **CASH FLOWS FROM OPERATING ACTIVITIES** | | | | |
| Cash received from user charges | $ 1,052,578 | $ 4,851,104 | $ 5,903,682 | — |
| Cash received from assessments made to other funds | — | — | — | $ 22,639,927 |
| Cash payments to employees for services | (888,793) | (10,494,786) | (11,383,579) | — |
| Cash payments for insurance claims | — | — | — | (22,639,927) |
| Cash payments to suppliers for goods and services | (35,449) | (7,855,737) | (7,891,186) | — |
| Cash payments for facility use | (826,746) | — | (826,746) | — |
| Cash payments for other operating expenses | — | (2,593) | (2,593) | — |
| Net cash used for operating activities | (698,410) | (13,502,012) | (14,200,422) | — |
| **CASH FLOWS FROM NONCAPITAL FINANCING ACTIVITIES** | | | | |
| Nonoperating grants received | 897,983 | 15,564,368 | 16,462,351 | — |
| **CASH FLOWS FROM CAPITAL AND RELATED FINANCING ACTIVITIES** | | | | |
| Capital contributions | — | 750,000 | 750,000 | |
| Acquisition of capital assets | — | (1,522,918) | (1,522,918) | — |
| Net cash used for capital and related financing activities | — | (772,918) | (772,918) | |
| **CASH FLOWS FROM INVESTING ACTIVITIES** | | | | |
| Interest on investments | 10,861 | 301,410 | 312,271 | — |
| Net increase in cash and cash equivalents | 210,434 | 1,590,848 | 1,801,282 | — |
| Cash and cash equivalents -- Beginning | 1,646,777 | 4,380,184 | 6,026,961 | — |
| Cash and cash equivalents -- Ending | $ 1,857,211 | $ 5,971,032 | $ 7,828,243 | — |
| Reconciliation of operating income (loss) to net cash provided (used) by operating activities: | | | | |
| Operating income (loss) | $ (901,603) | $ (15,845,682) | $ (16,747,285) | $ 1,224,659 |
| Adjustments to reconcile operating income (loss) to net cash provided (used) by operating activities: | | | | |
| Depreciation | — | 981,897 | 981,897 | — |
| Commodities used | — | 1,684,867 | 1,684,867 | — |
| Changes in assets and liabilities: | | | | |
| receivables | 97,996 | 100,754 | 198,750 | (2,549,089) |
| inventories | 113,226 | 210,239 | 323,465 | |
| accrued liabilities | (5,684) | (371,455) | (377,139) | 1,324,430 |
| deferred revenue | (2,345) | (262,632) | (264,977) | |
| **Net cash provided by operating activities** | **$ (698,410)** | **$ (13,502,012)** | **$(14,200,422)** | — |

**NONCASH NONCAPITAL FINANCING ACTIVITIES**
During the year the District received $1,684,867 of food commodities from the US Department of Agriculture.

## Fiduciary Funds Statements

The school district's fiduciary funds account for activity in which the school acts as a trustee or in an agency capacity for another party. These are resources that are not available to support district operations. There are four fiduciary fund types, which are pension (and other employee benefit) trust funds, investment trust funds, private purpose trust funds and agency funds (such as student activity funds). Therefore, fiduciary activities are not included in the district-wide statements because they represent resources that are not available for district operations. The two statements required for fiduciary funds are the statement of fiduciary net assets and statement of changes in fiduciary net assets. Figure 3-8 is an example of these statements, which are presented on the accrual basis of accounting. The fiduciary funds are presented by fund type rather than major funds. If the district has multiple funds, it may present combining statements for each of the fund types in its CAFR.

***Figure 3-8***
***Illustrative Statements of Fiduciary Net Assets and Illustrative Statement of Changes in Fiduciary Net Assets***

**ASBO International School District**
**Statement of Fiduciary Net Assets**
**As of June 30, 2002**

| | Private-Purpose Trust | Agency Funds |
|---|---|---|
| **ASSETS** | | |
| Cash and cash equivalents | $ 280,087 | $ 101,959 |
| Due from other governments | — | 100,242 |
| Accrued interest | 23,853 | — |
| Due from other funds | 321,026 | 1,272,211 |
| **Total assets** | **624,966** | **1,474,412** |
| **LIABILITIES** | | |
| Accounts payable | 1,450 | 14,911 |
| Due to student groups | — | 1,239,739 |
| Due to other governments | — | 219,762 |
| **Total liabilities** | **1,450** | **1,474,412** |
| **NET ASSETS** | | |
| Reserved for scholarships | 585,221 | |
| Unreserved | 38,295 | |
| **Total Net Assets** | **$623,516** | |

**ASBO, International School District**
**Statement of Changes in Fiduciary Net Assets**
**For the Year Ended June 30, 2002**

| | Private-Purpose Trusts |
|---|---|
| **ADDITIONS** | |
| Private donations | $ 24,480 |
| District contribution | 5,000 |
| Interest | 32,487 |
| Total additions | 61,967 |
| **DEDUCTIONS** | |
| Scholarships awarded | 36,644 |
| **Change in net assets** | **25,323** |
| Net Assets--Beginning | 598,193 |
| Net Assets--Ending | $ 623,516 |

## Budgetary Comparisons

A school district is required to prepare a budgetary comparison for its general fund and each major special revenue fund for which it legally adopts an annual budget. This may be done as a statement included as part of the basic financial statements or as a schedule included as required supplementary information. At a minimum, there will be three columns in this schedule or statement: original budget, final budget and actual data presented on the budgetary basis. A fourth and fifth column may be added to report the variance between the original budget and the final budget and the final budget to the actual results (see Figure 3-9).

***Figure 3-9***
***Illustrative Budgetary Comparison Statement***

**ASBO International School District**
**Budgetary Comparison Schedule for the General Fund**
**For the Year Ended June 30, 2002**

| | Budgeted Amounts | | Actual | Variances--Positive (Negative) | |
|---|---|---|---|---|---|
| | **Original** | **Final** | **(GAAP Basis)** | **Original to Final** | **Final to Actual** |
| **Revenues:** | | | | | |
| Property Taxes | $ 149,617,343 | $ 151,571,192 | $ 153,862,367 | $ 1,953,849 | $ 2,291,175 |
| Other Local Sources | 8,330,157 | 8,318,808 | 8,404,240 | (11,349) | 85,432 |
| Intermediate Sources | 1,773,000 | 1,885,500 | 2,106,451 | 112,500 | 220,951 |
| State Sources | 189,720,000 | 187,073,000 | 188,019,530 | (2,647,000) | 946,530 |
| Federal Sources | 2,137,500 | 2,250,000 | 2,284,748 | 112,500 | 34,748 |
| Other Sources | 364,500 | 364,500 | 395,088 | - | 30,588 |
| **Total revenues** | **351,942,500** | **351,463,000** | **355,072,424** | **(479,500)** | **3,609,424** |
| **Expenditures:** | | | | | |
| **Instruction:** | | | | | |
| Regular Instruction | 147,577,920 | 147,152,460 | 146,067,673 | 425,460 | 1,084,787 |
| Special Instruction | 34,288,430 | 34,189,580 | 33,937,539 | 98,850 | 252,041 |
| Other Instruction | 27,231,945 | 27,153,438 | 26,953,263 | 78,507 | 200,175 |
| **Total Instruction** | **209,098,295** | **208,495,478** | **206,958,475** | **602,817** | **1,537,003** |
| **Support Services:** | | | | | |
| Pupil Services | 34,413,082 | 34,694,864 | 34,010,001 | (281,782) | 684,863 |
| Instructional Staff Services | 12,185,382 | 12,411,520 | 12,579,165 | (226,138) | (167,645) |
| General Administration Services | 10,252,023 | 9,627,845 | 9,290,149 | 624,178 | 337,696 |
| Building Administration Services | 18,314,271 | 18,654,150 | 18,906,114 | (339,879) | (251,964) |
| Business Services | 6,442,400 | 6,442,400 | 6,047,066 | - | 395,334 |
| Operations & Maintenance | 35,078,360 | 35,432,695 | 33,258,353 | (354,335) | 2,174,342 |
| Pupil Transportation | 17,138,286 | 17,376,467 | 16,310,144 | (238,181) | 1,066,323 |
| Central Services | 1,725,361 | 1,721,536 | 1,691,107 | 3,825 | 30,429 |
| Principal and Interest | 1,531,812 | 1,531,812 | 1,538,918 | - | (7,106) |
| Other Support Services | 5,059,000 | 5,059,000 | 922,537 | - | 4,136,463 |
| **Total Support Services** | **142,139,977** | **142,952,289** | **134,553,554** | **(812,312.00)** | **8,398,735** |
| **Total expenditures** | **351,238,272** | **351,447,767** | **341,512,029** | **(209,495)** | **9,935,738** |
| Excess (deficiency) of revenues over expenditui | 704,228 | 15,233 | 13,560,395 | (688,995) | 13,545,162 |
| **SPECIAL ITEM** | | | | | |
| Proceeds from sale of unimproved land | 2,610,000 | 2,610,000 | 2,601,908 | — | (8,092) |
| **Net change in fund balances** | **3,314,228** | **2,625,233** | **16,162,303** | **(688,995)** | **13,537,070** |
| Fund balance--Beginning | 54,938,434 | 54,938,434 | 54,938,434 | — | — |
| Fund balance--Ending | $ 58,252,662 | $ 57,563,667 | $ 71,100,737 | $ (688,995) | $ 13,537,070 |

***ASBO recommends presenting budgetary comparison information as a required supplementary information schedule.*** The district is required to provide a reconciliation if the budget is prepared on a basis other than GAAP (See Figure 3-10). For example, if the school district's budget is prepared on a cash basis, it must reconcile this schedule (or statement) to the respective major governmental funds statement of revenues, expenditures, and changes in fund balances (Q 245,247- 253). If the budgetary comparison is presented as RSI, any excess of expenditures over budgeted appropriations in the individual funds is required to be disclosed in the notes (Q254).

***Figure 3-10***
***Illustrative Budgetary Comparison Reconciliation***

**Note A—Explanation of Differences between Budgetary Inflows and Outflows and GAAP Revenues and Expenditures for ASBO International School District**

| | General Fund | Special Revenue Fund |
|---|---|---|
| **Sources/inflows of resources** | | |
| Actual amounts (budgetary basis) "available for appropriation" from the budgetary comparison schedule | $92,370,775 | $ 4,349,914 |
| Differences—budget to GAAP: | | |
| The fund balance at the beginning of the year is a budgetary resource but is not a current-year revenue for financial reporting purposes. | (2,742,799) | (1,618,441) |
| Transfers from other funds are inflows of budgetary resources but are not *revenues* for financial reporting purposes. | (129,323) | — |
| The proceeds from the sale of the park land are budgetary resources but are regarded as a *special item,* rather than revenue, for financial reporting purposes. | (3,476,488) | — |
| Total revenues as reported on the statement of revenues, expenditures, and changes in fund balances—governmental funds. | $86,022,165 | $ 2,731,473 |
| **Uses/outflows of resources** | | |
| Actual amounts (budgetary basis) "total charges to appropriations" from the budgetary comparison schedule. | $90,938,522 | $ 3,314,572 |
| Differences—budget to GAAP: | | |
| Encumbrances for supplies and equipment ordered but not received is reported in the year the order is placed for *budgetary* purposes, but in the year the supplies are received for *financial reporting* purposes. | (186,690) | (16,037) |
| Transfers to other funds are outflows of budgetary resources but are not *expenditures* for financial reporting purposes. | (2,034,659) | (344,146) |
| Total expenditures as reported on the statement of revenues, expenditures, and changes in fund balances—governmental funds. | $88,717,173 | $ 2,954,389 |

# Chapter Four
# Capital Assets and Depreciation

GASB Statement 34 requires that districts issue district-wide financial statements using the economic resources measurement focus and accrual basis of accounting. In regard to capital assets, this requirement means that certain amounts reported in the fund financial statements will need to be restated for the district-wide statements. The restatement is necessary to adjust expenditures related to capital assets from the current financial resources measurement focus used in fund statements to the economic resources measurement focus used in the district-wide statements. In essence, the cost associated with the acquisition of capital assets will be replaced by the cost to use up the asset. The cost of usage, called depreciation, is reported in the current fiscal period in district-wide statements. This is contrasted with the cost of acquisition that is reported in the fund statements.

Statement 34 requires certain disclosures related to capital assets. Specifically, details by major classes should:

- present governmental activities separately from business-type activities
- report capital assets that are depreciated separately from those that are not
- report historical cost separately from accumulated depreciation.

For each class the following information, if applicable, should be reported:

- Beginning and end-of-year balances
- Acquisitions
- Sales or other dispositions
- Current depreciation expense.

Additionally, the amount of depreciation expense for each of the functions reported in the statement of activities must be disclosed.

To implement Statement 34, business officials will need to prepare for retroactive recognition of depreciation of capital assets as well as establish systems for prospective reporting.

To prepare for recognition of depreciation, the following tasks need to be performed:

1. Determine the level to which current capital asset records meet information needs necessary to comply with Statement 34.
2. Determine if there is a need to re-define capital assets (e.g. consider capitalization threshold), for purposes of compliance.
3. Determine the inventory of capital assets in service as of the effective date of Statement 34.
4. Review recent capital maintenance projects to ascertain those that should be capitalized.
5. Examine the historical or estimated historical cost for all capital assets. Valuations need to be objectively determined. Many districts will have asset values from the inception of the General Fixed Assets Account Group. Districts that choose to re-create records for Statement 34 compliance should consider the following information sources to assist with valuing the inventory.

   - Original purchase records
   - Bond documents
   - Professional appraisal or other services

6. Determine the year of purchase and the estimated useful life for existing capital assets.
7. Establish procedures to perpetuate the capital assets and depreciation system.
8. Determine the amount of accumulated depreciation at the implementation date and the amount of depreciation expense for the current period.
9. Determine salvage value, if any.

A capital asset is reported and, with certain exceptions discussed later in this chapter, depreciated in district-wide statements. In the district-wide statements, assets that are not capitalized are expensed in the year of acquisition.

## Asset Inventory (Q67)

School districts should develop strategies to ensure they have an accurate and up-to-date record of capital assets. School district should have such an inventory beginning in 1980 when NCGA Statement #1 created the General Fixed Assets Account Group. School districts without an inventory will need to have one prepared as of the start of the year in which Statement 34 is implemented. The district will need to devise a method to determine historical costs or estimated historical cost of capital assets on hand. The district will further need to establish a system to perpetuate the capital asset inventory. Future asset acquisitions will be valued at the acquisition cost for purchased items. Donated items will be capitalized at fair-market value on the donation date and depreciated if exhaustible over their remaining estimated useful lives.

School districts need to have an inventory of all capital assets. Each inventory record will need to include: description, year of acquisition, method of acquisition (e.g. purchase or donation), funding source, cost or estimated cost and estimated useful life. The inventory will also need to identify the function(s) that uses the asset. The inventory need only include those assets that meet the definition of a capital asset, as determined by the school district. (See Q233 about reporting assets by "class" of assets.)

Capital assets include sites (land), site improvements, buildings, building improvements, furniture, fixtures and equipment, vehicles, and other items that meet criteria established by the school district. Districts will need to consider several criteria when deciding what assets to capitalize.

### *Land (Q27, 34, 276)*

Land is not a depreciable asset. It is recorded at historical cost and remains at that cost until disposal. If there is a gain or loss on the sale or disposal of land, it is reported as a special item in the statement of activities.

### *Site Improvements (Q25)*

Site improvements include items such as excavation, non-infrastructure utility installation, driveways, sidewalks, parking lots, flagpoles, retaining walls, fencing, outdoor lighting, and other non-building improvements intended to make the land ready for its intended purpose. Depreciation of site improvements is necessary if the improvement is exhaustible. Expenditures for improvements that do not require maintenance or replacement, expenditures to bring land into condition to commence erection of structures, expenditures for improvements not identified with structures, and expenditures for land improvements that do not deteriorate with use or passage of time are additions to the cost of land and are generally not exhaustible and therefore not depreciable. Other improvements that are part of a site, such as parking lots, landscaping and fencing, are usually exhaustible and are therefore depreciable.

*Buildings and Construction in Progress (Q30-32, 34, 36-37)*

Buildings should be recorded at either their acquisition cost or construction cost. The cost of new construction should be carefully evaluated. Usually projects consist of major components such as land, land improvements, building construction (including professional fees and permits), furniture, fixtures and equipment. The value of each component needs to be determined because different useful lives and salvage values may apply. Further, interest paid during the construction of assets subsequent to Statement 34 is added to the construction cost.

Construction in progress should not be depreciated. It should be reported with land and other non-depreciating assets at the district-wide level. Unspent debt proceeds from capital assets-related debt should be reported in the net assets section of the statement of net assets as "restricted for capital projects." Refer to questions 89 and 90 of the GASB Guide to Implementation for further guidance in proper reporting of capitalized interest.

*Building Improvements*

Building improvements that extend the useful life should be capitalized. School districts should therefore review major maintenance projects for the last several years to determine those that should become part of the restatement of assets for purposes of complying with Statement 34.

Examples of building improvements include roofing projects, major energy conservation projects, or remodeling and replacing major building components. A district will need to determine the practicality of identification of these projects and prepare an inventory. The inventory will need to include a project description, the year completed, funding source and dollar amount. Only those projects that meet the capitalization threshold need to be included. Further, as a practical matter, districts should establish a cut-off date for retroactive recognition of site and facility improvements. ***ASBO recommends that districts review projects for the last three to five years unless meaningful data are readily available for preceding years.***

*Personal Property (Q26)*

Assets such as vehicles, furniture and equipment that meet threshold levels set by the district should be identified and inventoried. Some assets, individually, may fall below the capitalization threshold but may be purchased in large quantities by the district. Examples include library books, textbooks, and computers. Districts may choose to capitalize these assets as groups. ***ASBO recommends this be done if the assets are purchased with debt proceeds so that there is an asset to offset the debt on the statement of net assets.***

*Infrastructure*

Generally, school districts will have few, if any, infrastructure assets. Infrastructure assets are long-lived capital assets that normally can be preserved for a significantly greater number of years than most capital assets and that are normally stationary in nature. Examples include roads, bridges, tunnels, drainage systems, water systems, and dams. Infrastructure assets do not include buildings, drives, and parking lots or any of the other examples given above that are incidental to a school's property or access to the property. This guide does not address reporting requirements for infrastructure assets. If a school district determines it has these assets, the district should refer to GASB publications for guidance.

## Criteria for Determination of Capital Assets

*Estimated Useful Life*

The first criterion is useful life. An asset must have an estimated useful life greater than one reporting period to be considered for capitalization and depreciation. Assets that are consumed, used-up, habitually lost or worn-out in one year or less should not be capitalized.

Estimated useful life means the estimated number of months or years that an asset will be able to be used for the purpose for which it was purchased. In determining useful life, districts should consider the asset's present condition, use of the asset, construction type, maintenance policy, and how long it is expected to meet service demands. ***School districts are encouraged to adopt the standard useful life tables provided in this document.*** Notwithstanding, useful lives should be based on the district's own experience and plans for the assets. Although the standard useful life table presented here provides guidance, property management practices, asset usage, and other variables such as weather may require adjustment to the recommended lives. Schedules of depreciable lives established by federal or state tax regulations are generally not representative of useful lives.

School districts may choose to depreciate assets individually or by grouping assets. If the district elects to group assets, the estimated life of the group may be based on the weighted average or simple average of the useful life of individual items or on assessment of the life of the group as a whole. (See Appendix 4, Exercise #2 of the GASB Implementation Guide)

Periodically, the district should review the estimated remaining life of specific assets or groups of assets and adjust the remaining depreciable life accordingly. As with the determination of value, useful life can be determined by district staff or a professional appraiser (Q47-51).

Figure 4-1 represents guidelines ASBO developed to help school districts estimate useful lives of capital assets. The table is based on data developed by Valuation Resource Management (now VRM-MAXIMUS), a national property valuation firm. The ASBO committee adjusted portions of the VRM data and added several new classifications. The table should not be implemented without careful consideration of local factors that may impact an asset's useful life. Further, it is likely that school districts will have assets that are not included in the figure. For example, some districts may own cattle that they wish to capitalize. Each district is responsible for developing a rational system for identifying which assets to capitalize and their associated lives.

### *Asset Cost*

The second criterion for determining depreciable capital assets is cost (Q29). School districts do not need to capitalize every asset with a useful life greater than one year. To do so is an unnecessary burden and will not materially affect financial results. School districts may wish to establish a dollar threshold as a basis for considering an asset for capitalization. Care should be taken when determining the threshold. A threshold that is too low may result in a burdensome record-keeping system. A threshold that is too high could cause material misstatement of the district's financial condition. Consideration should be given to the diminishing returns of progressively lower capitalization levels. The above discussion is primarily intended to address the accounting threshold. School districts may choose to establish a different threshold for other purposes, such as control or insurance.

Exhibits A-1 through A-3, following, show the number of assets and total asset value for various capitalization thresholds for large, medium and small school districts. The exhibits illustrate that the number of assets is reduced significantly as the threshold increases. However, the total dollar value of capitalized assets is reduced only slightly. With a capitalization threshold of $5,000, large and medium-sized school districts would easily account for 80 percent of their assets. Small school districts will need a capitalization threshold of $1,000 to account for 80 percent of assets.

***Figure 4-1***

| Asset Class | Examples | Est. Useful Life in Years |
|---|---|---|
| Land | | N/A |
| Site Improvements | Paving, flagpoles, retaining walls, sidewalks, fencing, outdoor lighting | 20 |
| School Buildings | | 50 |
| Portable Classrooms | | 25 |
| HVAC Systems | Heating, ventilation, and air conditioning systems | 20 |
| Roofing | | 20 |
| Interior Construction | | 25 |
| Carpet Replacement | | 7 |
| Electrical/Plumbing | | 30 |
| Sprinkler/Fire System | Fire suppression systems | 25 |
| Outdoor Equipment | Playground, radio towers, fuel tanks, pumps | 20 |
| Machinery & Tools | Shop & maintenance equipment, tools | 15 |
| Kitchen Equipment | Appliances | 15 |
| Custodial Equipment | Floor scrubbers, vacuums, other | 15 |
| Science & Engineering | Lab equipment, scientific apparatus | 10 |
| Furniture & Accessories | Classroom and office furniture | 20 |
| Business Machines | Fax, duplicating & printing equipment | 10 |
| Copiers | | 5 |
| Communications Equip. | Mobile, portable radios, non-computerized | 10 |
| Computer Hardware | PCs, printers, network hardware | 5 |
| Computer Software | Instructional, other short-term | 5 to10 |
| Computer Software | Administrative or long-term | 10 to 20 |
| Audio Visual Equip. | Projectors, cameras (still & digital) | 10 |
| Athletic Equipment | Gymnastics, football, weight machines, wrestling mats | 10 |
| Musical Instruments | Pianos, string, brass, percussion | 10 |
| Library Books | Collections | 5 to 7 |
| Licensed Vehicles | Buses, other on-road vehicles | 8 |
| Contractors Equipment | Major off-road vehicles, front –end loaders, large tractors, mobile air compressor | 10 |
| Grounds Equipment | Mowers, tractors, attachments | 15 |

***Exhibit A-1***
***Large School District***

| Threshold | Number of Assets | Capitalized Value (in thousands) | Change |
|---|---|---|---|
| $1 | 50,000+ | $90,000 | |
| $300 | 9,529 | $87,329 | 3.0 percent |
| $500 | 7,196 | $86,376 | 4.0 percent |
| $1,000 | 4,384 | $84,444 | 6.2 percent |
| $2,000 | 2,235 | $81,022 | 10.0 percent |
| $5,000 | 478 | $76,075 | 15.5 percent |

***Exhibit A-2***
***Medium-Sized School District***

| Threshold | Number of Assets | Capitalized Value (in thousands) | Change |
|---|---|---|---|
| $1 | 12,000+ | $27,700 | |
| $300 | 2,476 | $26,786 | 3.3 percent |
| $500 | 2,065 | $26,619 | 3.9 percent |
| $1,000 | 1,304 | $26,059 | 5.4 percent |
| $2,000 | 360 | $24,736 | 10.7 percent |
| $5,000 | 167 | $24,175 | 12.7 percent |

***Exhibit A-3***
***Small School District***

| Threshold | Number of Assets | Capitalized Value (in thousands) | Change |
|---|---|---|---|
| $1 | | n/a | $2,929 |
| $300 | 896 | $2,830 | 3.4 percent |
| $500 | 608 | $2,723 | 7.0 percent |
| $1,000 | 324 | $2,521 | 13.9 percent |
| $2,000 | 98 | $2,189 | 25.3 percent |
| $5,000 | 36 | $2,007 | 31.5 percent |

**Data from the exhibits above were provided by VRM-MAXIMUS, a national appraisal firm.*

The Government Finance Officers Association (GFOA) suggests a capitalization threshold of an amount that ensures that at least 80 percent of the value of assets are reported, but the threshold should not be greater than $5,000. The federal government also uses a capitalization threshold of $5,000 for federal grant management purposes. The capitalization threshold chosen by the district will depend on a number of factors. School districts need to consider state regulations and guidelines, auditor interpretations, and the amount of associated debt, if any. ***ASBO recommends that school districts establish a capitalization threshold that ensures that at least 80 percent of the value of assets is reported; however the threshold should not be greater than $5,000.***

Improvements that extend the estimated useful life of sites or buildings should be capitalized. A higher capitalization threshold, such as $10,000 to $50,000, may be appropriate for these expenditures.

Prospective application of the requirement to capitalize and depreciate certain assets can be achieved by making certain that purchasing procedures provide for the collection of all necessary data. Information on the acquisition cost of an asset should be readily available. Acquisition cost includes shipping, set-up, and installation. Other costs, such as plumbing or electrical, incurred to place a new asset in service should be included in the asset's acquisition cost. Further, construction-period interest cost is to be capitalized as a component of historical cost (Q30-31).

Districts need to develop a means to objectively determine historical or estimated historical costs for assets owned by the district as of the effective date of Statement 34, if this had not been previously accomplished. Purchase records are generally the most accurate source of information. The cost to peruse and evaluate purchase records, except for the most recent years, is likely to be greater than the benefit achieved by having historical cost data. As an alternative,

- Districts should consider the services of a professional property appraisal firm. Property appraisal firms are able to perform the asset inventory, to provide estimated historical cost information, and to give an objective estimate of the asset's useful life that will generally be acceptable to auditors. The American Institute of Certified Public Accountants' Industry Audit Guide, *Audits of State and Local Governmental Units*, states "a government may use outside professional assistance to appraise property."
- It may also be suitable to use insurance valuations as a basis to assist with estimating historical cost.
- Often long-term debt is used to finance the purchase of capital assets. The total amount of original debt issuance may be an acceptable starting point to help determine some assets' historical cost (Q274).

***Associated Debt***

The third criterion is associated debt (Q274). School districts should carefully consider the merits of capitalizing assets purchased with debt proceeds. Doing so may minimize the potential of negative net assets being reported in the statement of net assets.

## Depreciation

In accounting terms, depreciation is the process of allocating the cost of tangible property over a period of time, rather than deducting the cost as an expense in the year of acquisition. Generally, at the end of an asset's life, the sum of the amounts charged for depreciation in each accounting period (accumulated depreciation) will equal original cost less salvage value. Good accounting and financial management practices require that a district take both the cost expiration and the declining value of an asset into consideration. The cost expiration of a district's assets must be recognized if the cost of providing services is to be realistically reported. Also, the decline in the value of those assets must be considered if the district's net assets are to be stated correctly.

To be depreciated, a capital asset must:

- be in use in the district
- have an estimated useful life greater than one year
- be subject to wear, decay, or expiration, and
- be fully installed and ready for use.

To calculate depreciation on a capital asset, the following five factors must be known:

- the date the asset was placed in service
- the asset's cost or acquisition value
- the asset's salvage value
- the asset's estimated useful life, and
- the depreciation method.

For general capital assets, depreciation is reported only on district-wide financial statements. Depreciation expense is reported on the Statement of Activities. Statement 34 requires that depreciation for assets specifically identified with specific functions is to be included in the direct expenses of those functions. Capital assets that serve essentially all functions, such as a high school, are reported on a separate line or reported as part of the general administration (or its counterpart) function. If depreciation is reported as a separate line item, the face of the statement must clearly indicate that this line item excludes depreciation expense charged to functions.

***ASBO recommends not allocating the depreciation of a building that serves multiple (that is, more than just a few) functions. However, if the district chooses to allocate, ASBO recommends that the allocation be based on square footage for the time used.***

Capital assets and the associated accumulated depreciation are reported in the statement of net assets. Accumulated depreciation may be reported separately, or capital assets may be presented net of accumulated depreciation on the statement. ***ASBO recommends reporting both the historical cost and accumulated depreciation in the face of the statement.***

The method used to calculate an asset's depreciation is important because depreciation reduces net assets. Accelerated depreciation methods reduce net assets more quickly than straight-line depreciation methods. In practical terms, depreciation suggests a gradual decline in an asset's value because of use. Statement 34 requires that school districts expense an amount each year that represents the cost of the actual use of the capital asset. This amount is treated as an expense even though the district may not have purchased the asset in the current period.

### *Averaging Conventions*

To avoid the complications of depreciating each asset from the specific date on which it was placed in service, GAAP supports guidelines that assume various assets are placed in service or disposed of at designated dates throughout the year. These guidelines are called averaging conventions.

There are five averaging conventions, as described below, in common use. ***ASBO recommends school districts use the full-month convention.*** The other conventions are described so business officials have an understanding of the available option.

Under a full-month convention, property placed in service at any time during a given month is treated as if it had been placed in service on the first of that month. This allows depreciation to be taken for the entire month in which the asset is placed in service. If the property is disposed of before the end of the estimated useful life, no depreciation is allowed for the month of disposition.

Under the half-year convention, an asset is treated as though it were placed in service or disposed of on the first day of the seventh month of the fiscal year. One-half of a full year's depreciation is allowed for the asset in its first year placed in service, regardless of when it was actually placed in service during that year. The half-year convention may be most appropriate for grouped assets such as library books or computers purchased throughout the year.

Under the modified half-year convention, assets placed in service during the first half of the year are considered to have been placed in service on the first day of the year. Therefore, they receive a full year's depreciation in the acquisition year. Assets placed in service during the second half of the year are considered to have been placed in service on the first day of the following year. Therefore, they receive no depreciation in the acquisition year but receive a full year's depreciation in the subsequent year.

Applying the modified half-year convention in the disposal year is slightly more complicated because the disposal-year allowance depends on the acquisition year allowance. The following table summarizes the relationships:

| If Asset Was Placed in Service in the: | And Disposed of in the: | Amount of Depreciation Allowed in the Disposal Year: |
|---|---|---|
| First half of year | First half of year | No depreciation |
| First half of year | Second half of year | 50 percent of full year depreciation |
| Second half of year | First half of year* | 50 percent of full year depreciation |
| Second half of year | Second half of year** | Full year of depreciation |

**Refers to a year subsequent to the year of acquisition.*
***To earn the full year of depreciation, the disposal must have been in a year after the acquisition year.*

ASBO urges caution with adopting this averaging convention for large capital assets due to the possibility that misstatement of asset values and depreciation could occur.

Under the *mid-month convention,* property is treated as though it were placed in service or disposed of in the middle of the month. A half-month's depreciation is allowed both in the month of acquisition and in the month of disposition. Generally this means that if the asset is placed in service after the 15th of the month, no depreciation is taken for that month. If the asset is placed in service on or before the 15th of the month, a full month's depreciation is allowed. Similarly, if the asset is disposed of on or before the 15th of the month, no depreciation is taken for that month. If the asset is disposed of after the 15th of the month, a full month's depreciation is allowed.

The *mid-quarter convention* treats property as though it were placed in service in the middle of the quarter in which it was purchased.

### Depreciable Cost

An asset's depreciable cost is the amount of the asset's value for which a district will claim depreciation. A percentage of this basis is deducted each year. The depreciable cost is often (but not always) the asset's cost or acquisition value. Under some depreciation methods, salvage value is considered in the determination of the depreciable cost.

One measure of an asset's depreciable cost is its purchase price. If something other than cash is used to pay for the asset, then the fair-market value of the non-cash payment or consideration determines the depreciable cost. A non-cash consideration often takes the form of an account payable or an obligation to pay. When the value of the consideration paid can't be determined, the asset's fair-market value determines its depreciable cost.

With few exceptions, an asset's depreciable cost should also include necessary costs incurred to place the asset in service. These costs will be capitalized, not expensed. Costs that should be capitalized include the invoice price plus incidental costs (insurance during transit, freight, capitalized interest as described earlier, duties, title search, registration fees, and installation costs). Exceptions to this rule include interest expenses associated with deferred payments and real estate taxes paid, if any, in the acquisition of property.

The salvage value of an asset is the value it is expected to have when it is no longer useful. In other words, the salvage value is the amount for which the asset could be sold at the end of its useful life.

Straight-line, sum-of-the-years'-digits, and some other depreciation methods require that the salvage value be subtracted from an asset's acquired value to determine its depreciable basis. Other methods, such as declining-balance, do not subtract the salvage value to determine the basis. However, the asset will not be depreciated below its salvage value.

### Depreciation Methods

There are many different methods used to calculate depreciation. Some methods allow more depreciation in early years than in later years. Some apply the same percentage each year while the basis declines. Others apply different percentages each year while the basis remains the same.

The same depreciation method is not required for all capital assets. Further, depreciation may be calculated for a class of assets, a group of assets or individual assets. Once a method for a particular asset is chosen, however, it must generally be used for the life of the asset. ***ASBO recommends school districts use the straight-line depreciation method.*** However, any established method of depreciation is acceptable by Statement 34. The straight-line depreciation method is described in greater detail below.

The straight-line method is the simplest and most commonly used for calculating depreciation. It can be used for any depreciable property. Under the straight-line depreciation method, the basis of the asset is written off evenly over the useful life of the asset. The same amount of depreciation is taken each year. In general, the amount of annual depreciation is determined by dividing an asset's depreciable cost by its estimated life.

The total amount depreciated can never exceed the asset's historic cost less salvage value. At the end of the asset's estimated life, the salvage value will remain.

For example, a $12,000 copier is placed in service on March 16, 2000. It has an estimated life of five years and a salvage value of $2,000. The depreciation calculation for the straight-line method would be:

| | |
|---|---|
| Original cost | $12,000 |
| Salvage value | $ 2,000 |
| Adjusted basis | $10,000 |
| Estimated life | 5 |
| Depreciation per year | $ 2,000 |

A full-year's depreciation would be $2,000. Under a full-month convention, property placed in service at any time during a given month is treated as if it had been placed in service on the first of that month. This permits depreciation for the entire month in which the asset is placed in service. If the property is disposed of before the end of the estimated useful life, no depreciation is allowed for the disposal month. The full-month convention allows depreciation for the month of March. The depreciation for the fiscal year ended June 30, 2000, would be 10/12ths of the annual depreciation or $1,666.67.

Under the mid-month convention, the copier is considered to be placed in service in April. Therefore, the depreciation for the fiscal year ended June 30, 2000, would be 9/12ths of the annual depreciation, or $1,500.

# Chapter Five
# Notes to the Financial Statements

The notes to financial statements provide additional information to the reader that has not been presented on the face of the financial statements (for reasons of practicality) but is essential for the financial statements to be fairly presented. This is why the phrase "The notes to the financial statements are an integral part of this statement" is included on the bottom of each basic financial statement. A district must determine which notes are necessary to ensure that the financial statements are fairly presented. Refer to the list in Figure 5-1 for examples of notes that may be applicable. GASB currently has a project to review note disclosures that may result in changes to required disclosures.

This chapter will highlight the major changes required by Statement 34. These changes affect the note disclosures for the summary of significant accounting policies, notes on capital assets and long-term liabilities and add detailed information to reconcile the fund financial statements to the district-wide statements, if necessary.

## Summary of Significant Accounting Policies

The changes in the summary of significant accounting policies are as follows:

- Description of district-wide statements, noting exclusion of fiduciary activity (Q230).
- Measurement focus and basis of accounting used in the district-wide and funds financial statements.
- Policy for eliminating internal activity in the district-wide statement of activities.
- Policy for applying FASB pronouncements to business type activities and to enterprise.
- Policy for capitalizing assets and for estimating the useful lives of those assets.
- Description of types of transactions included in program revenues.
- Policy for defining operating and non-operating revenues of proprietary funds.
- Policy regarding application of restricted resources when an expense is incurred for purposes for which both restricted or unrestricted net assets are available.
- Policy for allocating indirect expenses to functions in the district-wide statement of activities.

Remember, the notes explain the accounting methods and assumptions used by the school district when reporting financial transactions in its financial statements.

### *Capital Assets (Q232 and 233)*

One of the most significant changes a school district will encounter in implementing Statement 34 is depreciating its capital assets at the district-wide reporting level, which was discussed in Chapter Four. School districts are required to spread the cost of the assets over the assets' estimated useful lives. Therefore, more detailed information about the district's capital assets must be explained in the notes to financial statements (see Figure 5-2). Prior financial statements presented general fixed assets at cost or estimated historical cost until the assets were sold or destroyed. Under the new model, assets will be depreciated over their useful lives, and when an asset is sold, destroyed, or otherwise becomes unusable to the district, it will be removed from the capital asset and accumulated depreciation accounts. The depreciation expense amounts charged to each of the functions in the statement of activities should be disclosed.

***Figure 5-1***
***Selected Current Note Disclosures***

These two lists of note disclosures have been adapted from the GASB's *Codification of Governmental Accounting and Financial Reporting Standards.* Notes that are essential if the information in the financial statements is to be presented fairly include:

a. Summary of significant accounting policies
b. Cash deposits with financial institutions
c. Investments
d. Significant contingent liabilities (such as pending lawsuits or unfilled purchase orders)
e. Outstanding encumbrances
f. Significant effects of events subsequent to the end of the year
g. Annual pension cost and net pension obligations
h. Material violations of finance-related legal and contractual provisions
i. Future debt service requirements for currently outstanding debt
j. Commitments under operating leases
k. Construction and other significant commitments
l. Required disclosures about capital assets
m. Required disclosures about long-term liabilities
n. Deficit fund balance or net assets of individual funds
o. Receivables and payables between funds
p. Significant transactions between discretely presented component units and with the primary government
q. Disclosures about donor-restricted endowments

Additional note disclosures should be made if applicable to the government, including:

a. Risk management activities
b. Property taxes
c. Condensed financial statements for major discretely presented component units
d. Budget basis of accounting and budget-GAAP reporting differences not otherwise reconciled in the financial statements (Required only if schedule is presented as a basic statement.)
e. Short-term debt instruments and liquidity
f. transactions with related parties
g. The nature of the district's accountability for related organizations
h. Capital leases
i. Joint ventures and jointly governed organizations
j. Debt refunding (similar to refinancing a mortgage)
k. Methods of estimating fixed asset costs
l. Designations of fund balance amounts
m. Interfund eliminations in fund financial statements not apparent from headings
n. Pension plans
o. Bond, tax, or revenue anticipation notes excluded from fund or current liabilities (proprietary funds)
p. Nature and amount of inconsistencies in financial statements caused by transactions between component units having different fiscal year-ends or changes in component unit fiscal year-ends
q. Reverse repurchase and dollar reverse repurchase agreements
r. Securities lending transactions
s. Demand bonds
t. Post-employment benefits other than pension benefits (such as health insurance)
u. On-behalf payments for fringe benefits and salaries
v. Sponsoring government disclosures about external investment pools reported as investment trust funds
w. The amount of interest expense included in direct expenses (Q114)

***Figure 5-2***
***Illustrative Capital Assets Note Disclosure***

**Note 2—Disclosure of Information about Capital Assets**

Capital asset balances and activity for the year ended June 30, 2002 were as follows (in thousands):

| | Beginning Balance | Additions | Retirements/ Reclassifications | Ending Balance |
|---|---|---|---|---|
| **Governmental activities:** | | | | |
| Land | $ 22,059 | — | $ (1,235) | $ 20,824 |
| Construction in progress | 11,436 | $ 40 | — | 11,448 |
| Buildings | 250,090 | 674 | (10) | 250,754 |
| Furniture and equipment | 135,275 | 217 | (4,817) | 130,675 |
| Totals at historical cost | 418,860 | 931 | (6,062) | 413,701 |
| Less accumulated depreciation for: | | | | |
| Buildings | 61,547 | 11,345 | (10) | 72,882 |
| Furniture and equipment | 28,330 | 1,764 | (4,799) | 25,295 |
| Total accumulated depreciation | 89,877 | 13,109 * | (4,809) | 98,177 |
| **Governmental activities capital assets, net** | **$ 328,983** | **$ (12,178)** | **$ (1,253)** | **$315,524** |
| **Business-type activities:** | | | | |
| Furniture | $ 3,057 | $ 344 | — | $ 3,401 |
| Equipment | 6,881 | 1,267 | — | 8,148 |
| Totals at historical cost | 9,938 | 1,611 | — | 11,549 |
| Less accumulated depreciation for: | | | | |
| Furniture | 1,649 | 364 | — | 2,013 |
| Equipment | 6,385 | 618 | — | 7,003 |
| Total accumulated depreciation | 8,034 | 982 | — | 9,016 |
| **Business-type activities capital assets, net** | **$ 1,904** | **$ 629** | — | **$ 2,533** |

* Depreciation expense was charged to governmental functions as follows:

| | |
|---|---|
| Depreciation not allocated to specific functions | $ 6,555 |
| Instruction | 4,106 |
| Pupil Services | 587 |
| General Administration Services | 653 |
| School Administration Services | 164 |
| Operations & Maintenance of Plant Services | 996 |
| Transportation | 48 |
| **Total** | **$ 13,109** |

### *Long-Term Liabilities*

A note in the financial statements should explain in detail a school district's long-term debt (see Figure 5-3 and Q234). Governmental and business-type activities are shown separately with major categories of long-term liabilities listed (e.g. general bonded debt, lease purchase, notes payable, compensated absences, termination pay, claims and judgments). The district should present the beginning balance, additions, reductions, ending balance, and amount due within one year in columnar format. The amount due within one year will tie to the district-wide statement of net assets as the "current portion of long-term obligations." The note should also disclose which governmental funds typically have been used to liquidate other long-term liabilities in prior years (Q234)

***Figure 5-3***
***Illustrative Long-Term Debt Note Disclosure***

**Note 3—Disclosure of Information about Long-term Liabilities**

Long-term liability balances and activity for the year ended June 30, 2002 were as follows (in thousands):

| | Beginning Balance | Additions | Reductions | Ending Balance * | Amounts Due within One Year |
|---|---|---|---|---|---|
| **Governmental Activities** | | | | | |
| General Obligation Debt | | | | | |
| Bonds & Notes Payable | $ 108,221 | — | $ 11,710 | $ 96,511 | $ 12,875 |
| Lease-purchase obligations | 2,029 | $ 692 | 1,356 | 1,365 | 1,063 |
| Contractual obligations | 3,765 | — | 461 | 3,304 | 461 |
| Total general obligation debt | 114,015 | 692 | 13,527 | 101,180 | 14,399 |
| Other liabilities: | | | | | |
| Accumulated termination pay | 18,885 | 7,906 | 10,300 | 16,491 | 1,961 |
| Claims and judgments | - | - | - | - | - |
| Compensated absences | 1,060 | 327 | 261 | 1,126 | 195 |
| Total other liabilities | 19,945 | 8,233 | 10,561 | 17,617 | 2,156 |
| Total long-term liabilities | $ 133,960 | $ 8,925 | $ 24,088 | $118,797 | $ 16,555 |

* Payments on bonds and notes payable are made by the debt service fund. The accumulated termination pay and compensated absences liabilities will be liquidated by several of the governmental funds. The claims and judgments liability will generally be liquidated by the workers compensation internal service fund.

Statement 34 requires a summary reconciliation of the governmental fund statements to the district-wide statements. These reconciliations must be presented on the face of the fund statements or in a schedule following the statement. The balance sheet reconciles fund balance with the net assets of the governmental activities. The statement of revenues, expenditures, and changes in fund balance reconciles net change in fund balance with the change in net assets of governmental activities. More detailed reconciliations may need to be included in the notes to financial statements (see Figure 5-4 & 5-5; Q 189, 190, 191, and 218; Appendix 4-Exercise 6). GASB states "if aggregated information in the summary reconciliation obscures the nature of the individual elements of a particular reconciling item, governments should provide a more detailed explanation in the notes to financial statements." ***ASBO's recommendation regarding a separate reconciliation schedule may preclude the necessity of a detailed note disclosure.***

The notes to the financial statements provide necessary disclosure of material items, the omission of which would cause the financial statements to be misleading. The suggested areas to be considered for notes, as listed above, are neither all-inclusive nor intended to replace the professional judgment of district officials in determining if additional disclosures are necessary. This assessment must be balanced, however, by a desire not to clutter the notes and thereby make them difficult to comprehend.

*Figure 5-4*
***Illustrative Note Disclosure Reconciling the Governmental Funds, Balance Sheet with the District-wide Statement of Net Assets***

**Note 5—Explanation of Differences between Governmental Funds Balance Sheet and the Statement of Net Assets**

Total fund balances of the District's governmental funds ($74,630,486) differs from "net assets" of governmental activities ($290,563,158) reported in the statement of net assets. This difference primarily results from the additional long-term economic focus of the statement of net assets versus the solely current financial resources focus of the governmental fund balance sheets.

**Balance Sheet/Statement of Net Assets**

| | Total Governmental Funds | Long-term Assets, Liabilities [a] | Internal Service Funds [b] | Reclassifications and Elimination's | Statement of Net Assets Totals |
|---|---|---|---|---|---|
| **ASSETS** | | | | | |
| Cash and cash equivalents | $ 106,268,980 | — | — | — | $ 106,268,980 |
| Property taxes receivable (net) | 12,182,730 | — | — | — | 12,182,730 |
| Due from other governments | 19,968,336 | — | — | — | 19,968,336 |
| Due from other funds | 7,782,292 | — | $ 17,589,312 | $ (24,756,007) | 615,597 |
| Other receivables | 2,252,919 | — | — | — | 2,252,919 |
| Inventories and other assets | 1,537,230 | — | — | — | 1,537,230 |
| Capital assets | — | $ 315,524,231 | — | — | 315,524,231 |
| **Total assets** | **$149,992,487** | **$ 315,524,231** | **$ 17,589,312** | **$ (24,756,007)** | **$458,350,023** |
| **LIABILITIES** | | | | | |
| Accounts payable and other current liabilities | $ 31,712,117 | $ — | $ 11,566,721 | $ 1,593,237 | $ 44,872,075 |
| Due to other funds | 26,349,244 | — | — | (26,349,244) | — |
| Matured bonds and interest payable | 0 | | — | | 0 |
| Deferred revenue | 15,300,640 | (12,182,730) | — | — | 3,117,910 |
| Long-term liabilities | — | 118,796,880 | — | — | 118,796,880 |
| Total liabilities | 73,362,001 | 106,614,150 | 11,566,721 | (24,756,007) | 166,786,865 |
| **FUND BALANCES/NET ASSETS** | | | | | |
| Total fund balances/net assets | 76,630,486 | 208,910,081 | 6,022,591 | — | 291,563,158 |
| **Total liabilities and fund balances/net assets** | **$149,992,487** | **$ 315,524,231** | **$ 17,589,312** | **$ (24,756,007)** | **$ 458,350,023** |

[a] The costs of building and acquiring capital assets (land, buildings, equipment) financed from the governmental funds are reported as expenditures in the year they are incurred, and the assets do not appear on the balance sheet. However, the statement of net assets includes those capital assets among the assets of the district as a whole, and their original costs are expensed annually over their useful lives.

| | |
|---|---|
| Original cost of capital assets | $ 413,701,452 |
| Accumulated depreciation | (98,177,221) |
| | $ 315,524,231 |

Because the governmental funds focus on short-term financing, some assets will not be available to pay for current-period expenditures. Those assets (for example, receivables) are offset by deferred revenue in the governmental funds and thus are not included in fund balance. They are, however, included in the net assets of the governmental activities.

| | |
|---|---|
| Adjustment of deferred revenue | $ 12,182,730 |

Long-term liabilities are reported in the statement of net assets but not in the governmental funds because they are not due and payable in the current period. Balances at June 30, 2002 were:

| | |
|---|---|
| Bonds and notes payable | $ 101,179,845 |
| Compensated absences | 1,125,955 |
| Accumulated termination pay | 16,491,080 |
| Subtotal, long-term liabilities | $ 118,796,880 |

[b] Internal service funds are used by management to charge the costs of certain activities, such as insurance and telecommunications, to individual funds of the district. The assets and liabilities of the internal service funds, which are reported in the proprietary funds rather than the governmental funds, are included in governmental activities in the statement of net assets.

***Figure 5-5***
***Illustrative Note Disclosure Reconciling the Government Funds Statement of Revenues, Expenditures, and Changes in Fund Balances with the District-wide Statement of Activities***

**Note 6—Explanation of Differences between Governmental Funds Operating Statement and the Statement of Activities**

Total revenues and other financing sources ($408,174,460) in the governmental funds differ from total revenues for governmental activities ($406,764,735) in the statement of activities. The differences result primarily from the economic focus of the statement of activities versus the current financial resources focus of the governmental funds. The main components of the difference are described below.

Total revenues and other financing sources of the governmental funds consist of:

| | | | |
|---|---|---|---|
| Revenues | | $ | 404,880,307 |
| Proceeds from capital leases | | | 692,245 |
| Proceeds from sale of land | | | 2,601,908 |
| Total revenues and other sources—governmental funds | | | 408,174,460 |

| | |
|---|---|
| Because some property taxes will not be collected for several months after the District's fiscal year ends, they are not considered as "available" revenues in the governmental funds. | 517,087 |
| The proceeds from the sale of land ($2,601,980) are reported as revenue (as a special item) in the governmental funds. However, the cost of the land sold ($1,235,000) is removed from the capital assets account in the statement of net assets and offset against the sale proceeds resulting in a "gain on sale of land" in the statement of activities. Thus, the revenue reported in the governmental funds is greater than the gain in the statement of activities. | (1,234,567) |
| Some of the assets acquired this year were financed with capital leases. The amount financed by the leases is reported in the governmental funds as a source of financing. However, capital leases are not revenues in the statement of activities, but long-term liabilities in the statement of net assets. | (692,245) |

Total revenues of governmental activities in the statement of activities consist of:

| | | | |
|---|---|---|---|
| Charges for services | $ 8,495,891 | | |
| Operating grants and contributions | 42,270,310 | | |
| General revenues and special item | 355,998,534 | | |
| Total revenues of governmental activities | | **$** | **406,764,735** |

Total expenditures ($391,033,289) of the governmental funds differ from total expenses of governmental activities ($387,689,545) reported in the statement of activities. The difference is attributable primarily to the economic focus of governmental activities versus the current financial resources focus of governmental funds. The main components of the differences are described below.

| | | |
|---|---|---|
| Total expenditures reported in Governmental Funds | $ | 391,033,289 |
| In the statement of activities, certain operating expenses--compensated absences (vacations) and special termination benefits (early retirement)--are measured by the amounts *earned* during the year. In the governmental funds, however, expenditures for these items are measured by the amount of financial resources used (essentially, the amounts actually *paid* ). This year, special termination benefits paid ($10,300,426) *exceeded* the amounts earned ($7,906,074) by $2,394,352. Vacation used ($261,132) was *less than* the amounts earned ($327,280) by $66,148. | | (2,328,204) |
| When the purchase or construction of capital assets is financed through the governmental funds, the resources expended for those assets are reported as expenditures in the years they are incurred. However, in the statement of activities the cost of those assets is allocated over their estimated useful lives and reported as depreciation expense. This is the amount by which depreciation ($13,108,809) exceeded capital expenditures ($930,864) in the current ŗ | | 12,177,945 |
| An internal service fund is used by management to charge the costs of unemployment insurance to individual funds. The governmental funds expenditures include the $23,864,586 that the internal service fund charged. The expenses of the governmental activities, however do not reflect the amount paid, but the actual cost of the insurance ($22,639,927). The difference represents an overcharge by the internal service fund that is allocated back to the governmental activities. | | (1,224,659) |
| Repayment of bond principal is an expenditure in the governmental funds, but it reduces long-term liabilities in the statement of net assets and does not affect the statement of activities. | | (13,526,946) |
| Interest on long-term debt in the statement of activities differs from the amount reported in the governmental funds because interest is recorded as an expenditure in the funds when it is due, and thus requires the use of current financial resources. In the statement of activities, however, interest expense is recognized as the interest accrues, regardless of when it is due. The additional interest reported in the statement of activities is the net result of two factors. First, accrued interest on bonds, leases, and contracts payable *decreased* by $43,380. Second, $1,601,500 of additional accumulated interest was accreted on the district's "capital appreciation" bonds. | | 1,558,120 |
| Total expenses of governmental activities | **$** | **387,689,545** |

# Chapter Six
# The Comprehensive Annual Financial Report

Many school districts publish a comprehensive annual financial report (CAFR). A CAFR (Q 158 and 246) is a district's official annual financial report, containing the basic financial statements as well as introductory material; additional statements and schedules; and other financial, economic and demographic information. The information in the CAFR combining individual non-major fund statements and schedules is useful to show fund data in more detail than is presented in the basic financial statements.

Statement 34 does not change the CAFR requirements. Accordingly, the basic CAFR triad of introductory, financial, and statistical sections is still required.

The contents of the three sections include:

- Introductory section, including a letter of transmittal
- Financial section, which includes the auditor's report, Management's Discussion and Analysis (MD&A), basic financial statements, required supplemental information (RSI), combining and individual fund financial statements and schedules
- Statistical section

## Introductory Section

The introductory section is the CAFR's first major section. As the name implies, this section introduces the reader to the CAFR. It provides an overview of the annual report. It includes the following:

- Cover
- Title Page
- Table of Contents
- Transmittal Letter
- Certificate of Excellence Award (if applicable)
- Listing of Board Members and Administrators
- Organizational Chart

The transmittal letter describes the school district's organizational and management structure as well as the general policies and procedures. This letter is important for those who may not read the entire document.

The school district may want to supplement items in the financial statements with other relevant information not covered elsewhere in the CAFR. The transmittal letter should not duplicate information that is required to be reported in the MD&A. If the district previously prepared a CAFR, the transmittal letter will need to be modified as a result of Statement 34 so it will not duplicate the same information. The transmittal letter will still contain information not required in the MD&A. It may also complement, reinforce, and/or reference information that is now reported in the MD&A. The MD&A is considered to be RSI, and as such, its requirements take precedence over the transmittal letter.

ASBO's Certificate of Excellence (COE) Program (see Appendix B) establishes the following criteria in the ASBO self-evaluation worksheet for the transmittal letter.

The transmittal letter should be:

a. presented on the school district's letterhead stationery
b. dated on or after the date of the auditor's report
c. signed by both the chief financial officer and the chief executive officer (may include others at the school's option).

The transmittal letter should include, but not be limited to, discussions of the following subjects:

a. Management responsibility for financial information
b. Explanation of CAFR sections
c. Definition of the reporting entity
d. Internal controls
e. Budgetary controls
f. Cash management
g. Risk management
h. Independent audit with scope limitations discussed
i. Certificate of Excellence
j. Acknowledgments
k. Service efforts and accomplishments

The transmittal letter should be consistent with those in the other CAFR sections. The COE Award is valid for only one year. Thus, if a school received the COE in Financial Reporting for its preceding CAFR, the introductory section should include a copy of that year's certificate. The listing of board members and administrators and organizational chart can be displayed in any of a number of ways.

## Financial Section

The financial section consists of the MD&A, the auditor's report, the basic financial statements including notes to financial statements, RSI, and the combining and individual fund financial statements, and should include the following:

1. The MD&A is presented before the basic financial statements. It introduces the basic financial statements and includes an analytical overview of the school district's financial activities (See Chapter 1).
2. Auditor's opinion letter.
3. The basic financial statements are the heart of the school district's comprehensive annual financial report, consisting of the district-wide statements, fund statements, and notes to the financial statements.
4. RSI – Besides the MD&A discussed above, the school district is required to present budgetary comparison schedules, if not presented as a basic statement.
5. Combining and individual fund financial statements and schedules consist of the following:
   a. Combining Statements
      (i) By non-major fund, when the school district has more than one non-major fund.
      (ii) For discretely presented component units, when the reporting entity has more than one component unit (major component units should be presented in the basic statements or notes).
   b. Individual Fund Statement, when a school district wants to present prior-year and budgetary comparisons.

c. Schedules, when a school district wants to present schedules necessary to demonstrate compliance with finance-related legal and contractual provisions or schedules to summarize information presented throughout the statements that can be brought together and shown in greater detail (for example, taxes receivable, including delinquent taxes; long-term debt; investments; cash receipts, disbursements; and balances).

## Statistical Section

The CAFR's last section is the statistical section, which presents comparative data for several periods of time, most often 10 years. This section may contain data from sources other than the accounting records. These sources should be indicated on each schedule. The use of graphs is beneficial to readers of this section. At a minimum, the COE Program criteria requires the following information in this CAFR section:

a. General school district expenditures by function-last 10 fiscal years
b. General school district revenues by source-last 10 fiscal years
c. Property tax levies and collections-last 10 fiscal years
d. Assessed and estimated actual value of taxable property-last 10 fiscal years
e. Property tax rates-all direct and overlapping governments-last 10 fiscal years
f. Ratio of net general bonded debt to assessed value and net bonded debt per capita-last 10 fiscal years
g. Computation of legal debt margin
h. Computation of direct and overlapping debt
i. Ratio of annual debt service expenditures for general bonded debt to total general expenditures-last 10 fiscal years
j. Revenue Bond Coverage-last 10 fiscal years
k. Demographic Statistics-last 10 fiscal years
l. Property Values, Construction, and Bank Deposits-last 10 fiscal years
m. Principal taxpayers
n. Miscellaneous statistics

Although listed above, the revenue bond coverage tables are not commonly found in school district CAFRs.

In addition to the tables listed above, other information may be presented in the statistical section. Examples include:

a. Annual average FTE
b. Student enrollment and attendance data
c. Food service operations
d. Operational expenditures by pupil
e. Per-pupil expenditure ranking
f. Schedule of insurance and surety bonds in force

# Appendix A
# Sample Management Discussion and Analysis
# (Modified from GASB School District User Guide)

*Adapted from material in a working draft from the Government Accounting Standards Board, tentatively titled "What You Should Know About Your School District's Finances: A Guide to Financial Statements."*

This section of ASBO International School District's annual financial report presents its discussion and analysis of the district's financial performance during the fiscal year ending June 30, 2002. Please read it in conjunction with the transmittal letter at the front of this report and the district's financial statements, which immediately follow this section.

## Financial Highlights

- The district's financial status improved substantially for the second year in a row. Total net assets increased more than 7 percent over the course of the year.
- Overall revenues were $430 million, fully $20 million more than expenses.
- The total cost of basic programs rose 2.3 percent to $388 million. Because the portion of those costs paid for with charges, fees, and intergovernmental aid increased, the net cost that required taxpayer funding grew just 1.2 percent to $337 million.
- The net assets of our business-type activities – food services and adult education – increased more than 11 percent. Revenues increased 15 percent to $24 million while expenses increased 11 percent to $22 million.
- Food services began a much-needed modernization this year, adding $1.6 million of new equipment and furniture.
- Enrollment in the vocational and high school equivalency programs increased 12 percent to its highest level ever. The tuition-based continuing education course offerings doubled to 25.
- Outlays for new capital assets were low because the planned opening of two new school buildings was postponed until next year due to construction delays. Maintenance and operations spending also was significantly below budget as a result.
- The district reduced its outstanding long-term debt $13 million or 11 percent.

## Overview of the Financial Statements

This annual report consists of three parts: management's discussion and analysis (this section), the basic financial statements, and required supplementary information. The basic financial statements include two kinds of statements that present different views of the district:

- The first two statements are *district-wide financial statements* that provide both *short-term* and *long-term* information about the district's *overall* financial status.
- The remaining statements are *fund financial statements* that focus on *individual parts* of the district, reporting the district's operations in *more detail* than the district-wide statements.
- The *governmental funds statements* tell how basic services such as regular and special education were financed in the *short term* as well as what remains for future spending.

- *Proprietary funds* statements offer *short-* and *long-term* financial information about the activities the district operates *like businesses,* such as food services.
- *Fiduciary funds* statements provide information about the financial relationships in which the district acts solely as a *trustee* or *agent* for the benefit of others.

The financial statements also include notes that explain some of the information in the statements and provide more detailed data. The statements are followed by a section of required supplementary information that further explains and supports the financial statements with a comparison of the district's budget for the year. Figure A-1 shows how the various parts of this annual report are arranged and related to one another.

***Figure A-1***
***Organization of ASBO International School District Annual Financial Report***

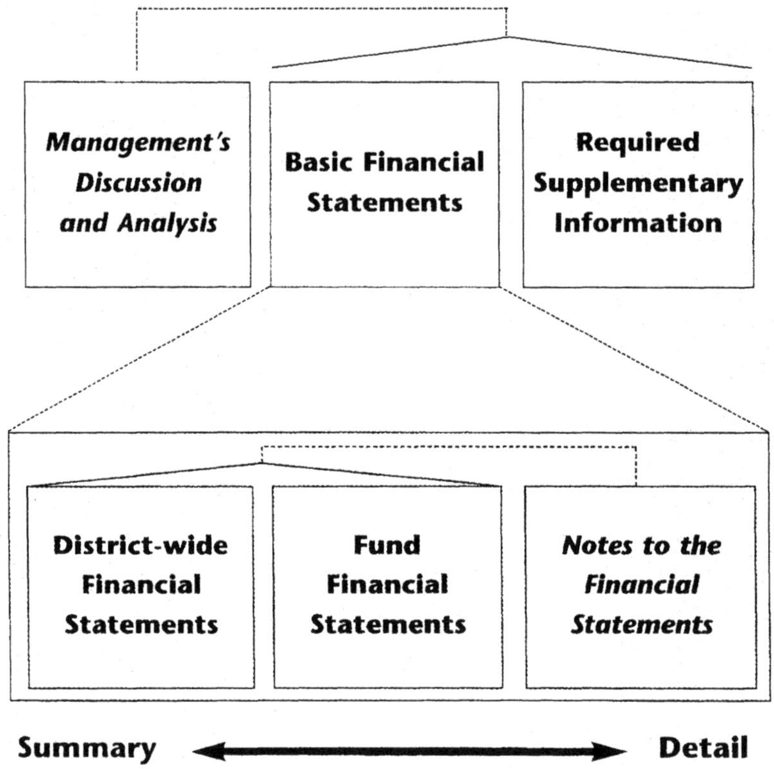


Figure A-2 summarizes the major features of the district's financial statements, including the portion of the district's activities they cover and the types of information they contain. The remainder of this overview section of management's discussion and analysis highlights the structure and contents of each of the statements.

***Figure A-2***
***Major Features of the District-Wide and Fund Financial Statements***

| | District-wide Statments | Fund Financial Statements | | |
|---|---|---|---|---|
| | | Governmental Funds | Proprietary Funds | Fiduciary Funds |
| Scope | Entire district (except fiduciary funds) | The activities of the district that are not proprietary or fiduciary, such as special education and building maintenance | Activities the district operates similar to private businesses: food services and adult education | Instances in which the district adminsters resources on behalf of someone else, such as scholarship programs and student activities monies |
| Required financial statements | • Statement of net assets<br>• Statement of activities | • Balance sheet<br>• Statement of revenues, expenditures, and changes in fund balances | • Statement of net assets<br>• Statement of cash flows | • Statement of diduciary net assets<br>• Statement of changes in fiduciary net assets |
| Accounting Basis and measurement focus | Accural accounting and economic resources focus | Modified accrual accounting and current financial focus | Accrual accounting and economic resources focus | Accrual accounting and economic resources focus |
| Type of asset/ liability information | All assets and liabilities, both financial and capital, short-term and long-term | Generally assets expected to be used up and liabilities that come due during the year or soon thereafter; no capital assets or long-term liabilities included | All assets and liabilitites, both financial and capital, and short-term and long-term | All assets and liabilities, both short-term and long-term; funds do not currently contain capital assets, although they can |
| Type of inflow/out flow information | All revenues and expenses during year, regardless of when cash is received or paid | Revenues for which cash is received during or soon after the end of the year; expenditures when goods or services have been received and the related liability is due and payable | All revenues and expenses during the year, regardless of when cash is sreceived or paid | All additions and deductions during the year, regardless of when cash is received or paid |

***District-wide Statements***

The district-wide statements report information about the district as a whole using accounting methods similar to those used by private-sector companies. The statement of net assets includes all of the district's assets and liabilities. All of the current year's revenues and expenses are accounted for in the statement of activities regardless of when cash is received or paid.

The two district-wide statements report the district's *net assets* and how they have changed. Net assets – the difference between the district's assets and liabilities – is one way to measure the district's financial health or *position*.

- Over time, increases or decreases in the district's net assets are an indicator of whether its financial position is improving or deteriorating, respectively.
- To assess the district's overall health, you need to consider additional non-financial factors such as changes in the district's property tax base and the condition of school buildings and other facilities.

In the district-wide financial statements, the district's activities are divided into two categories:

- *Governmental activities:* Most of the district's basic services are included here, such as regular and special education, transportation, and administration. Property taxes and state formula aid finance most of these activities.
- *Business-type activities:* The district charges fees to help it cover the costs of certain services it provides. The district's adult education programs and food services are included here.

### *Fund Financial Statements*

The fund financial statements provide more detailed information about the district's funds, focusing on its most significant or "major" funds – not the district as a whole. Funds are accounting devices the district uses to keep track of specific sources of funding and spending on particular programs:

- Some funds are required by state law and by bond covenants.
- The district establishes other funds to control and manage money for particular purposes (such as repaying its long-term debts) or to show that it is properly using certain revenues (such as federal grants).

The district has three kinds of funds:

- *Governmental funds:* Most of the district's basic services are included in governmental funds, which generally focus on (1) how cash and other financial assets that can readily be converted to cash flow in and out and (2) the balances left at year-end that are available for spending. Consequently, the governmental funds statements provide a detailed short-term view that helps you determine whether there are more or fewer financial resources that can be spent in the near future to finance the district's programs. Because this information does not encompass the additional long-term focus of the district-wide statements, additional information at the bottom of the governmental funds statements explains the relationship (or differences) between them.
- *Proprietary funds:* Services for which the district charges a fee are generally reported in proprietary funds. Proprietary funds are reported in the same way as the district-wide statements. The district's *enterprise funds* (one type of proprietary fund) are the same as its business-type activities but provide more detail and additional information, such as cash flows. The district uses *internal service funds* (the other kind of proprietary fund) to report activities that provide supplies and services for the its other programs and activities. The district currently has one internal service fund, the workers' compensation fund.
- *Fiduciary funds:* The district is the trustee, or *fiduciary*, for assets that belong to others, such as the scholarship fund and the student activities funds. The district is responsible for ensuring that the assets reported in these funds are used only for their intended purposes and by those to whom the assets belong. The district excludes these activities from the district-wide financial statements because it cannot use these assets to finance its operations.

## Financial Analysis of the District as a Whole

Net assets. The district's *combined* net assets were significantly larger on June 30, 2002, than they were the year before, increasing more than 7 percent to $304.0 million. (See Figure A-3.) Most of this improvement in the district's financial position came from its governmental activities, the net assets of which grew $19.1 million to $291.6 million. The net assets of the district's business-type activities increased $1.3 million to $12.4 million; although the dollar growth was smaller, it nonetheless represented an increase of more than 11 percent.

***Figure A-3***
***Condensed Statement of Net Assets (in millions of dollars)***

| | Governmental Activities | | Business-type Activities | | Total School District | | Total Percentage Change |
|---|---|---|---|---|---|---|---|
| | 2001 | 2002 | 2001 | 2002 | 2001 | 2002 | 2001-2002 |
| Current and other assets | $ 117.8 | $ 142.8 | $ 9.9 | $ 11.2 | $ 127.7 | $ 154.0 | 20.6% |
| Capital assets | 329.1 | 315.5 | 1.9 | 2.5 | 331.0 | 318.1 | -3.9% |
| **Total assets** | **446.9** | **458.4** | **11.8** | **13.7** | **458.7** | **472.1** | **2.9%** |
| Long-term debt outstand | 134.0 | 118.8 | - | - | 134.0 | 118.8 | -11.3% |
| Other liabilities | 40.4 | 48.0 | 0.7 | 1.3 | 41.1 | 49.3 | 20.0% |
| Total liabilities | 174.4 | 166.8 | 0.7 | 1.3 | 175.1 | 168.1 | -4.0% |
| Net assets | | | | | | | |
| Invested in capital assets, net of related debt | 219.2 | 231.1 | 1.9 | 2.5 | 221.1 | 233.7 | 5.7% |
| Restricted | 6.0 | 5.5 | - | - | 6.0 | 5.5 | -7.5% |
| Unrestricted | 47.3 | 54.9 | 9.2 | 9.9 | 56.6 | 64.8 | 14.5% |
| **Total net assets** | **$ 272.5** | **$ 291.6** | **$ 11.1** | **$ 12.4** | **$283.6** | **$ 304.0** | **7.2%** |

*Note: totals may not add due to rounding.*

The district's improved financial position is the product of many factors. Growth during the year in taxes and grants was a significant contributor to this improvement. Another notable factor was a construction workers strike that delayed the planned opening of two new school buildings – Common Middle School and Basic High School for the Arts – until next year. Consequently, about $2 million of expected maintenance and operations costs related to the new buildings did not arise.

Changes in net assets. The district's total revenues (excluding a special item) increased 4 percent to $429.1 million. (See Figure A-4.) Property taxes and state formula aid accounted for most of the district's revenue, with each contributing about 40 cents of every dollar raised. (See Figure A-5.) Another 14 percent came from state and federal aid for specific programs and the remainder from fees charged for services and miscellaneous sources.

The total cost of all programs and services rose 2.7 percent to $410.1 million. The district's expenses are predominantly related to instructing, caring for (pupil services) and transporting students (74 percent). (See Figure A-6.) The district's administrative and business activities accounted for 11 percent of total costs. The most significant contributor to the higher costs was maintenance and operations expenses, which increased $900,000 or 3.1 percent, due primarily to salary increases for custodial and security personnel and higher fuel costs due to a particularly cold winter. The nearly $6 million increase in instructional costs also derives largely from salary increases, in this case for teachers and other educational staff.

Total revenues (including the gain from an unused lot the district sold) surpassed expenses, increasing net assets $20.4 million over last year. Both the governmental and business-type activities contributed to the district's healthier fiscal status.

***Figure A-4***
***Changes in Net Assets from Operating Results (in millions of dollars)***

| | Governmental Activities | | Business-type Activities | | Total School District | | Total Percentage Change |
|---|---|---|---|---|---|---|---|
| | 2001 | 2002 | 2001 | 2002 | 2001 | 2002 | 2001-2002 |
| **Revenues** | | | | | | | |
| Program revenues | | | | | | | |
| Charges for services | $ 7.9 | $ 8.5 | $ 5.0 | $ 5.7 | $ 12.9 | $ 14.2 | 10.2% |
| Operating Grants & Contributions | 38.3 | 42.3 | 15.3 | 17.0 | 53.7 | 59.3 | 10.4% |
| Capital Grants & Contributions | | | | 0.7 | - | 0.7 | |
| General revenues | | | | | | | |
| Property taxes | 162.8 | 171.0 | - | - | 162.8 | 171.0 | 5.0% |
| State formula aid | 175.0 | 176.3 | - | - | 175.0 | 176.3 | 0.7% |
| Other | 6.8 | 7.4 | 0.3 | 0.3 | 7.0 | 7.7 | 9.5% |
| **Total revenues** | **390.8** | **405.4** | **20.6** | **23.7** | **411.4** | **429.1** | **4.3%** |
| **Expenses** | | | | | | | |
| Instruction | 228.9 | 234.8 | | | 228.9 | 234.8 | 2.6% |
| Pupil & Instructional Services | 44.8 | 44.0 | | | 44.8 | 44.0 | -1.8% |
| Administration & Business | 43.7 | 41.4 | | | 43.7 | 41.4 | -5.3% |
| Maintenance & operations | 29.5 | 30.4 | | | 29.5 | 30.4 | 3.1% |
| Transportation | 8.8 | 8.6 | | | 8.8 | 8.6 | -2.3% |
| Other | 23.4 | 28.5 | 20.2 | 22.4 | 43.6 | 50.9 | 16.7% |
| **Total expenses** | **379.1** | **387.7** | **20.2** | **22.4** | **399.3** | **410.1** | **2.7%** |
| Excess (deficiency) before special item | 11.7 | 17.7 | 0.4 | 1.3 | 12.1 | 19.0 | 56.9% |
| Special item: land sale | - | 1.4 | - | - | - | 1.4 | - |
| **Increase (decrease) in net asset:** | **$ 11.7** | **$19.1** | **$ 0.4** | **$1.3** | **$12.1** | **$20.4** | **68.2%** |

*Note: totals may not add due to rounding.*

***Figure A-5***
***Sources of Revenues for Fiscal Year 2002***

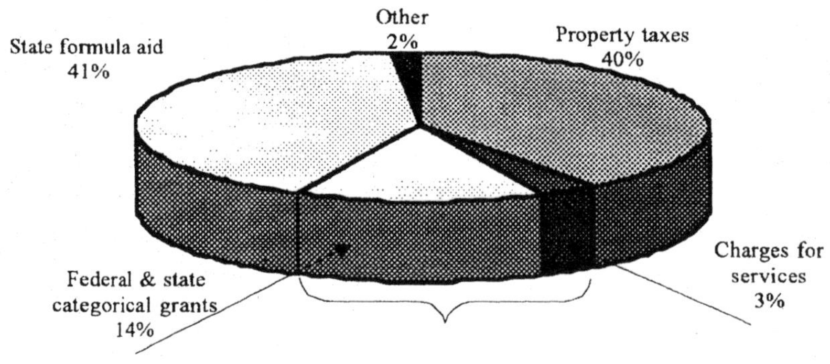

***Figure A-6***
***Expenses for Fiscal Year 2002***

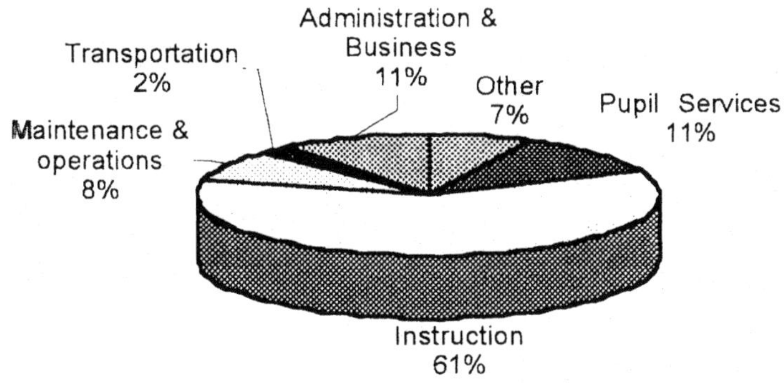


### *Governmental Activities*

Revenues for the district's governmental activities (excluding the land sale) increased 3.7 percent, while total expenses increased 2.3 percent. With the gain on the sale of the land, the increase in net assets for governmental activities was $19.1 million in 2002. This was the second consecutive year that net assets increased substantially, following an $11.7 million increase in 2001.

The recent good health of the district's finances can be credited both to a strong economy and innovative management changes:

- Rising real estate values led to a 5 percent increase in property tax revenues, despite the fact that tax rates remained unchanged. The district has not raised tax rates since 1997. Operating grants and contributions for governmental activities increased 10.4 percent to $42.3 million.
- The district sold a vacant parcel of land for $2.6 million, for a gain (net of the $1.2 million originally paid) of $1.4 million. The district originally purchased the land in 1988 as a site for a new school to replace Common Middle School's aging building. The district ultimately decided to construct the new school nearby on Common's current campus. Although the district did not need the proceeds from the sale to finance services this year, the decision to sell the land this year was based on the availability of a buyer and the district's judgment that a better offer was not likely to be received in the near future. This sale was a one-time occurrence; the district has no further plans to sell other assets, and therefore future budgets will not count on these resources recurring.
- The district is in the second year of implementing the Superintendent's Efficiency and Effectiveness (SEE) Plan. The goal of the SEE Plan is to initiate changes that reduce the cost of operating the district and reinvest the savings in programs to modernize and raise the quality of education. The actions taken thus far include:
- Redrawing bus routes to reduce the total number of routes and buses needed.
- Shifting non-pedagogical personnel to free teachers from administrative tasks.
- Contracting out some services previously provided to individual schools by the central district office.

These actions resulted in savings of approximately $3 million in 2002. The district will begin to use these savings in 2003 for projects agreed upon by a committee of school-based and central district teaching, support, supervisory, and administrative personnel.

Figure A-7 presents the cost of six major district activities: instruction, pupil and instructional services, administration and business, maintenance and operations, transportation, and other. The table also shows each activity's *net cost* (total cost less fees generated by the activities and intergovernmental aid provided for specific programs). The net cost shows the financial burden placed on the district's taxpayers by each of these functions.

***Figure A-7***
***Net Cost of Governmental Activities (in millions of dollars)***

| | Total Cost of Services | | Percentage Change | Net Cost of Services | | Percentage Change |
|---|---|---|---|---|---|---|
| | 2001 | 2002 | 2001-2002 | 2001 | 2002 | 2001-2002 |
| Instruction | $ 228.9 | $ 234.8 | 2.6% | $ 197.3 | $ 201.6 | 2.2% |
| Pupil & Instructional Services | $ 44.8 | $ 44.0 | -1.8% | 36.3 | 36.1 | -0.6% |
| Administration & Business | $ 43.7 | $ 41.4 | -5.3% | 39.2 | 36.8 | -6.1% |
| Maintenance & operations | $ 29.5 | $ 30.4 | 3.1% | 26.7 | 27.5 | 3.0% |
| Transportation | $ 8.8 | $ 8.6 | -2.3% | 7.6 | 7.8 | 2.6% |
| Other | $ 23.4 | $ 28.5 | 21.8% | 25.7 | 27.1 | 5.4% |
| **Total** | **$379.1** | **$387.7** | **2.3%** | **$ 332.8** | **$ 336.9** | **1.2%** |

*Note: totals may not add due to rounding.*

- The cost of all *governmental* activities this year was $387.7 million.
- Some of the cost was financed by the users of the district's programs ($8.5 million).
- The federal and state governments subsidized certain programs with grants and contributions ($42.3 million).
- Most of the district's costs ($336.9 million), however, were financed by district and state taxpayers.
- This portion of governmental activities was financed with $171 million in property taxes, $176.3 million of unrestricted state aid based on the statewide education aid formula, and investment earnings.

### *Business-Type Activities*

Revenues of the district's business-type activities increased 15 percent to $23.7 million, and expenses rose 10.9 percent to $22.4 million. (Refer to Figure A-4.) Factors contributing to these results included:

- Food services revenues exceeded expenses by $1.1 million, accounting for most of the increase in the net assets of the business-type activities. At the start of the school year in September 2001, food services raised prices 5 percent across the board with the intention of building resources to replace and modernize its old and obsolete kitchen equipment. The district also received a state capital grant of $750,000 to help defray the modernization costs. During the year $1.6 million of new equipment and furniture was purchased, and additional purchases will be made next year using the surplus resources from this year.
- The adult education program was dramatically expanded in 2002:

1. The grant-supported high school equivalency and vocational training courses served 3,500 adults, up 12 percent from the prior year and the highest enrollment since the program's inception.
2. The number of tuition-based continuing education courses doubled from 12 to 25, with a total enrollment of nearly 900 for the year.

## Financial Analysis of The District's Funds

The strong financial performance of the district as a whole is reflected in its governmental funds as well. As the district completed the year, its governmental funds reported combined fund balances of $76.6 million, well above last year's ending fund balances of $59.5 million.

All but one of the district's governmental funds had more revenues than expenditures in 2002, thereby contributing to the increase in total fund balance. Most significantly, $3.5 million of planned capital outlays connected with the opening of two new schools did not take place because of a construction strike. The only fund that ran a deficit was the family assistance fund, a special revenue fund that records the use of block grant money received from the state for providing parenting and counseling services to the parents of disadvantaged students. Expenditures of that fund were approximately $658,000 above revenues because some unused resources from last year were used this year to finance expenditures.

As mentioned, the business-type activities also did well financially. In addition to the district-wide financial statements, food services and the adult education program are reported in greater detail in the proprietary funds statements. In 2002, both services took steps that were important to district finances:

- Enrollment in the adult education courses grew rapidly, especially among the courses that charge a fee to participants. This growth has an impact on the governmental funds, because the program pays the district for the classroom and administrative space it utilizes. In 2002, the program's facility rental cost was $827,000.
- The equipment used by food services is old and, in some cases, obsolete. Despite adding $1.6 million of new equipment and furnishings in 2002, food services' capital assets were 78 percent depreciated. A 5 percent price increase on all menu items was enacted as part of an effort to raise the resources necessary to modernize and replace the old equipment, and the state provided a grant of $750,000.

### *General Fund Budgetary Highlights*

Over the course of the year, the district revised the annual operating budget several times. These budget amendments fall into two categories:

- Changes made in the third and fourth quarters to account for the postponed opening of two new school facilities and for higher-than-expected property tax revenues.
- Increases in appropriations to prevent budget overruns.

Although the district's final budget for the general fund anticipated that revenues and expenditures would be roughly equal, the actual results for the year show a $13.6 million surplus.

- Actual revenues were $3.6 million higher than expected, due largely to the property tax and some unexpected state aid.
- The actual expenditures were $9.9 million below budget, due primarily to the delayed opening of the new school buildings:
- Budgeted capital outlays of $5.1 million were actually $923,000 for the year; virtually all of the difference is accounted for by the final payments on the school construction.
- Actual expenditures for maintenance and operations of school facilities were more than $2 million below budgeted levels.

## Capital Asset and Debt Administration

*Capital Assets*

By the end of 2002, the district had invested $318 million in a broad range of capital assets, including school buildings, athletic facilities, computer and audio-visual equipment, and administrative offices. (See Figure A-8.) This amount represents a net decrease of $12.8 million or 3.9 percent from last year. (More detailed information about capital assets can be found in Note 2 to the financial statements.) Total depreciation expense for the year exceeded $14 million, and land originally costing $1.3 million was sold, while building improvements and additions to equipment and furniture amounted to just $2.5 million.

***Figure A-8***
***Capital Assets (net of depreciation, in millions of dollars)***

| | Governmental Activities | | Business-type Activities | | Total School District | | Total Percentage Change |
|---|---|---|---|---|---|---|---|
| | 2001 | 2002 | 2001 | 2002 | 2001 | 2002 | 2001-2002 |
| Land | $ 22.1 | $ 20.8 | - | - | $ 22.1 | $ 20.8 | -5.6% |
| Construction in progress | 11.4 | 11.4 | - | - | 11.4 | 11.4 | 0.4% |
| Buildings | 188.5 | 177.9 | - | - | 188.5 | 177.9 | -5.7% |
| Equipment & furniture | 106.9 | 105.4 | $ 1.9 | $ 2.5 | 108.8 | 107.9 | -0.9% |
| Total | $ 329.0 | $315.5 | $ 1.9 | $ 2.5 | $ 330.9 | $318.1 | -3.9% |

*Note: totals may not add due to rounding.*

The district had expected to complete the two school buildings this year, but construction difficulties have delayed their opening until next year. ASBO's student enrollment has grown steadily over the last three years, 9 percent since 1999 to reach a present enrollment of 73,650. Since 1996, student enrollment has exceeded the district's seating capacity. When complete, the two state-of-the-art school facilities will provide 7,000 additional seats, bringing the district's capacity to nearly 75,000.

The district's fiscal year 2003 capital budget projects spending another $6 million for capital projects, principally in two areas:

- $4 million to complete the new facilities for Common Middle School and Basic High School.
- $1.5 million to continue the modernization of the food service equipment.

***Long-Term Debt***

At year-end, the district had $101 million in general obligation bonds and other long-term debt outstanding – a reduction of 11 percent from last year – as shown in Figure A-9. (More detailed information about the district's long-term liabilities is presented in Note 2 to the financial statements.)

***Figure A-9***
***Outstanding Long-Term Debt (in millions of dollars)***

| | Total School District 2001 | Total School District 2002 | Total Percentage Change 2001-2002 |
|---|---|---|---|
| General obligation bonds & note (financed with property taxes) | $ 108.2 | $ 96.5 | -10.8% |
| Other general obligation debt | 5.8 | 4.7 | -19.0% |
| Total | $ 114.0 | $ 101.2 | -11.2% |

- The district continued to pay down its debt, retiring $13.5 million of outstanding bonds.
- Only $692,000 in new debt was issued during the year.

The district plans to issue about $4 million in new bonds in 2003 to pay for the completion of the new school buildings. The district will continue to pay cash, however, for the additional food services equipment rather than finance the equipment with long-term debt.

## Factors Bearing on the District's Future

At the time these financial statements were prepared and audited, the district was aware of four existing circumstances that could significantly affect its financial health in the future:

- The end of fiscal year 2002 marked the expiration of the last three-year teachers' contract. A new three-year labor agreement was approved in August 2002. The economic package (salaries and fringe benefits) contained in the new contract provides for 4 percent annual increases. This contract will increase the district's costs $6.6 million in 2003, $13.5 million in 2004, and $20.7 million in 2005.
- The district is plaintiff with other urban school districts in a lawsuit against the state, seeking to rectify inequities in the formula the state uses to apportion education aid to the districts. The district is requesting an additional $40 million of state aid annually.
- The district was a defendant in a lawsuit brought by one of its largest taxpayers. Spehr Tire, Inc. consolidated its manufacturing operations in its main factory in another state and closed its local plant. The company asked that the assessed value of the now-empty factory be cut drastically to reflect that the property is no longer being used and, Spehr contended, is not capable of generating income for the company. The court decided in favor of Spehr, costing the district about $4 million in annual property tax revenues.
- In 2004, the district must implement the more stringent academic standards mandated by the State Education Board's Total Educational Accountability Reforms (TEARs). TEARs may result in a smaller percentage of students being

promoted to the next grade each year and a lower percentage of students graduating from high school. If this were to occur, the district's pupil enrollment would rise. It is not possible at this time to predict what will happen if promotion and graduation rates decline, but based on current costs, every 1 percent enrollment increase would raise instructional costs approximately $2 million annually, not including the cost of support services, transportation, and administration.

## Contacting the District's Financial Management

This financial report is designed to provide the district's citizens, taxpayers, customers, and investors and creditors with a general overview of the district's finances and to demonstrate the district's accountability for the money it receives. If you have questions about this report or need additional financial information, contact the Controller's Office, ASBO International School District, 14 Pavilion Road, Reston, VA 22090.

# Appendix B
# The ASBO Certificate of Excellence in Financial Reporting Program

The Certificate of Excellence in Financial Reporting program was designed by the Association of School Business Officials (ASBO) International to encourage excellence in the preparation and issuance of school district comprehensive annual financial reports (CAFRs). A Certificate of Excellence is awarded to school districts that have submitted their CAFR and, upon completion of a technical review, are judged by the review panel members to have satisfied the criteria for excellence in financial reporting. The Certificate of Excellence Award is the highest form of recognition in school financial reporting issued by ASBO International.

ASBO established the COE Program in 1972 and currently receives applications from more than 400 school districts and community-supported educational institutions located throughout the United States. Since certificates are granted based on a particular fiscal year's report, a school district must resubmit its CAFR annually to maintain its certificate.

## Benefits To Participants In The Certificate of Excellence Program

***Prestigious National Award***

Since its inception, the program has gained the distinction of being a prestigious national award recognized by:

- Accounting professionals
- Bond counsels
- Underwriters
- Securities analysts
- Educational, teacher and citizen groups
- Federal and state agencies

***Validates Fiscal Credibility***

Receipt of a Certificate of Excellence validates a school district's fiscal and financial management credibility with its various reporting constituencies, including:

- School board members, superintendents
- School district management
- State and Local Government agencies
- Oversight entities
- State and federal granting agencies
- Education, taxpayer and teacher organizations

***Enhances Report Presentations***

Inclusion of a Certificate of Excellence enhances a school district's financial presentations in:

- Annual Reports
- Bond issuance official statements
- Presentations to the media
- Budget presentations and hearings
- Continuing disclosure requirements

### *Provides a Measure of Uniformity*

Adherence to the formatting and terminology as promulgated by the appropriate standard-setting bodies (GASB, AICPA, etc.) allows for comparability between:

- School districts
- School district reports from year to year

### *Offers Individual Recognition and Development*

Receipt of a Certificate of Excellence provides a school district's board and superintendent with a measure of the integrity and technical competence of the system's fiscal administration. Participation in this landmark program is an unparalleled professional experience.

## Submitting a CAFR for Review

Participating school districts submit their CAFR and application materials within six months of their fiscal year end. The application must include:

- One copy of the Official Certificate of Excellence Application Form
- Three copies of the school district's CAFR
- Three copies of the school district's responses to the prior year's comments (if applicable)
- Three copies of the Self-Evaluation Worksheet (Submitting the worksheet is optional for school districts that received the award for the prior fiscal year. New applicants, past conditional awards, and past denials are required to complete and submit three copies of the worksheet.)
- Payment based on the total revenue of all funds

Send application, with materials and payment, to: ASBO International, Certificate of Excellence Program, 11401 North Shore Drive, Reston, VA 20190-4200.

To request program information and application materials, contact ASBO International, 11401 North Shore Drive, Reston, VA 20190-4200 • Phone: (703) 478-0405• Fax: (703) 478-0205 • Web site: *www.asbointl.org*.

***ASBO International Accounting, Auditing and Budgeting Committee Subcommittee on GASB Statement No. 34 Implementation***

Nicholas C. A. Alioto, CPA
Assistant Superintendent of Business
Kenosha Unified School District No 1
Kenosha, WI
*nalioto@kusd.edu*

Denny G. Bolton, Ph.D., RSBA
Business Administrator/Board Secretary
Owen J. Roberts School District
Pottstown, PA
*dbolton@ojr.k12.pa.us*

E. Danny Cash, RSBA
Assistant Superintendent – Finance and Operations
Community Consolidated School District 21
Wheeling, IL
*dcash@d21.k12.il.us*

Roger J. Dickson, RSBA
Assistant Superintendent for Business
Kettle Moraine School District
Wales, WI
*roger@kmsd.edu*

Gary Heinfeld, CPA
Managing Partner
Heinfeld & Meech P.C. CPAs
Tuscon, AZ
*gary@heinfeldmeech.com*

George M. Lingel
Assistant Superintendent for Business
Community Consolidated School District 15
Palatine, IL
*lingelg@esc.ccsd15.k12.il.us*

Jack W. McKelvy, RSBA
Executive Director of Support Services
Mesa County School District #51
Grand Junction, CO
*jmckelvy@mesa.k12.co.us*

***ASBO Staff Liaisons***

Linda Prevatte
Director of Professional Development

Don I. Tharpe, Ed.D.
ASBO Executive Director

***Technical Editors***

Edward Blaha
Deputy Director
Georgia Department of Audits and Accounts
Atlanta, GA
*Blahaef@audits.state.ga.us*

Tim Green, CPA
Partner
Allen, Green & Company, LLP
Monroe, LA
*tim@allengreencpa.com*

W. Gary Harmer, CPA
Assistant Superintendent of Business Services
Salt Lake City School District
Salt Lake City, UT
*gary.harmer@slc.k12.ut.us*

George Scott
Partner
Deloitte & Touche, LLP
Fort Worth, TX
*gscott@dttus.com*

ASBO would like to acknowledge and express its appreciation to the GASB staff, particularly David Bean, Randy Finden, Dean Mead, and Ken Schermann, for their assistance in editing this guide and providing their technical assistance and advice. In addition, ASBO acknowledges the assistance of Mark Hessel of VRM-MAXIMUS in developing the Asset Life Figure.

www.ingramcontent.com/pod-product-compliance
Ingram Content Group UK Ltd.
Pitfield, Milton Keynes, MK11 3LW, UK
UKHW051417150926
475561UK00005B/219

9 781578 860678